SHOCK
THE
WHEAT

HELPING JESUS SEEK AND SAVE THE LOST

G. JACK WREN

CROSSBOOKS

CrossBooks™
A Division of LifeWay
One LifeWay Plaza
Nashville, TN 37234
www.crossbooks.com
Phone: 1-866-768-9010

All Scripture quotations are taken from the Disciple's Study Bible: New
International Version, copyright 1988 by Holman Bible Publishers.

First published by CrossBooks 7/29/2014

ISBN: 978-1-4627-3911-0 (sc)
ISBN: 978-1-4627-3913-4 (hc)
ISBN: 978-1-4627-3912-7 (e)

Library of Congress Control Number: 2014912344

Printed in the United States of America.

This book is printed on acid-free paper.

Any people depicted in stock imagery provided by Thinkstock are models,
and such images are being used for illustrative purposes only.
Certain stock imagery © Thinkstock.

CONTENTS

ACKNOWLEDGMENTS

I thank Beth, my first mentor, who lovingly prayed for me, patiently waited for God's work of grace in me, and provided more than a half century of faithful support in the ministry to which God called us. I am eternally indebted to hundreds of others, most of whom must, because of the passing of time, remain anonymous. I thank Jan, the second love of my life, for her suggestions in the first drafts, and my good friend, Josh Smith, for his expertise in grammar and encouragement to continue the work. I am also grateful to my grandson, Lance Wren, and to Ricky Waller for their patient reading and their corrections.

However, my greatest thanks are to my loving heavenly Father, who would not let me go. God patiently revealed nuggets of truth, building on them to bring me into the circle of His family. Holy Father, may this book excite praise for You, may it give hope to Your servants, and may it inspire some, who perhaps are resting on the bench, to get in the race of life with You.

INTRODUCTION

. . . .

God told the prophet Isaiah, "Your ways are not my ways ... my ways are higher than your ways" (Isaiah 55:8–9). What do God's higher ways look like? How does He work in people's lives to bring them to acceptance of His existence, belief in Jesus' work on the cross, and submission to the leadership of the Holy Spirit? *Shock the Wheat* details the way God used a wheat field, a cemetery, a tent, a quarter hour, a hospital room, a midnight word, and a book discovery to make one man a "fisher of men."

Soon after I became a Christian, God called me to preach, and I said no. I have learned that God did not take my no seriously. He knew that my no to Him came from spiritual ignorance, born of immaturity and a total lack of knowledge of the Bible. However, God can overcome spiritual ignorance because He has a beautiful plan for every person. God's plan always leads us to fall in love with Him, and when we do we will hear Him say, in one form or another, "Whom shall I send? And who will go for us?" We will cry out in loving appreciation, "Here am I. Send me" (Isaiah 6:8).

Oh, may all who come behind us find us faithful;

may the fire of our devotion light their way;

may the footprints that we leave lead them to believe,

and the lives we live inspire them to obey.

—Anonymous

My prayer is that you too will discover the providential hand of God. I hope you will learn with me that none of us is beyond God's reach and that He never abandons His plan for His children. May God help each of us to remember the times, perhaps long since forgotten, when God poured His grace into our lives. May this renewing memory encourage each of us to be about the task of shocking God's wheat in His harvest field.

This book is a testimony to the providence of God, the patient persistence of the Holy Spirit, the power in the Word of God to change a person's life, and the blessedness of the purpose of God when it unfolds in obedient living and in joyful ministry.

Heavenly Father, remind us of the times in our lives when You were so real and poured on us Your bountiful blessings. May these memories serve as reminders in the same way the twelve stones Joshua erected reminded the Israelites that they were in the Promised Land by the mighty hand of God (Joshua 4:19–24). Please use these memories to humble us, to increase our faith, and to deepen our commitment to You. Amen!

CHAPTER 1

THE JOURNEY BEGINS

In the beginning God created the heavens and the earth ...
Then God said, let us make man in our image, in our likeness.

—Genesis 1:1, 26

. . . .

Shock the Wheat was born on a hot summer day in the early 1940s. This was the first of many identifying moments in my life. It's been said that sometimes you never know the value of a moment until it becomes a memory.

Wheat must be planted to produce a harvest. Likewise, a seed of faith in God must be planted to bring about a spiritual harvest. My life with God began like a planted seed, and God has used many of His chosen people to cultivate and water His work in my life. (See 1 Corinthians 3:5–9.)

Life in the hills of eastern Kentucky in the early 1940s had changed little in the past one hundred years. One- and two-room schoolhouses identified local communities. Spring plowing, tobacco-bed burning, and crop planting dictated that school be in session from July to February. Fields were plowed, planted, and harvested with horse-drawn equipment. In our community, power-driven farm machinery was limited to a steel-tired tractor. There was however, a gas-powered thrashing machine and a hay bailer, both of which were stationary.

I think it was 1943 when Dad planted a field of wheat. When harvested, wheat was first cut by a horse-drawn binder. The binder then rolled the wheat into bundles, tied the bundles, and dropped them in the field. The bundled wheat was then stood upright in round shocks measuring about six feet across. Once the wheat was in shocks, a wide- mouth rake was used to move it to the thrasher. There the bundled wheat was hand fed into the thrasher, which separated the wheat grains from the straw.

Dad was riding the binder, and I was helping him shock the wheat. I was eleven and had to wrestle the bundles of wheat to get them to the shock. The day was hot and sticky, sweat bees were stinging, and since I wore only cut-off bibbed overalls and no undershirt, the wheat heads made me itch. I stopped my father and said, "Dad, it is too hot to shock wheat! The sweat bees are stinging me, and the wheat heads make me itch." Dad was chewing tobacco, and he squirted a stream of tobacco juice over the wheel and said, "What does it being hot, sweat bees stinging, and the wheat itching you have to do with the price of eggs in China?"

This was not what I wanted to hear, and I replied, "What has the price of eggs in China got to do with it being hot, sweat bees stinging, and wheat itching?" He looked me in the eye and said, "Not a thing. Shock the wheat!" I shocked wheat all that day. I have only lately begun to realize the impact my dad's words had on my life. I deeply regret that I had not thought through, while he was alive, the lesson Dad taught me that day in the wheat field. Thanks Dad, because the title of this book belongs to you.

I am persuaded that the words "shock the wheat" came from the heart of God. As I contemplated writing this book, I realized for the first time the effect Dad's words had on me. I know he was saying harvest time had arrived and the ripe wheat had to be harvested. However, there was a greater lesson in those words. They spoke to taking care of business and staying focused on the important issues of life. Dad was saying, in his way, what the writer of Hebrews said: "Let us throw off everything that hinders and the sin that so easily entangles, and run with perseverance the race marked out for us" (Hebrews 12:1). Keeping at the task Jesus assigns is very much like shocking wheat. There is an urgency concerning the harvest, and difficult side effects must not be allowed to interfere with Christ's assignment.

The Christian life is filled with many distractions, but there is one essential truth. Jesus is the way to the Father's house (John 14:14). Therefore we must keep our eyes on the Good Shepherd and follow in His footsteps.

John 21:15–23 is the account of Jesus reinstating Peter. Keep in mind that one English word may be used to translate several Greek words. A case in point is the dialogue between Jesus and Peter. Their conversation went something like this. Jesus asked Peter two times, "Do you truly love me?" (John 21:15–16). The Greek word for love that Jesus used was *agape*. This is God's kind of self-giving love. Peter answered both times, "Yes, Lord you know that I love you" (John

21:15–16). The Greek word Peter used was *phileo*, and this means brotherly love, a huge step down from God's kind of love.

The third time, Jesus said, "Simon son of John, do you love me?" (John 21:17). In this exchange, Jesus used *phileo*, Peter's word for love. It seems as though Peter was reluctant to overstate his feelings for the Lord, so he said, "Lord, you know that I love [phileo] you" (John 21:17). Many biblical scholars think that Jesus asked Peter if he loved Him three times because Peter had denied knowing Him three times. We do not know for sure why the Lord posed the question three times, but we do know that following each of Peter's answers, Jesus assigned him a ministering task.

Jesus also told Peter the kind of death he would experience (John 21:18) at which time Peter looked around and saw that John was following them. Peter said to Jesus, "Lord, what about him?" (John 21:2). Jesus replied, "What is that to you? You must follow me" (John 21:22). In light of Jesus' command to Peter, my dad's words, "Shock the wheat," become eternally important.

We must keep in mind that the encounter between Jesus and Peter took place during the forty days between the Lord's resurrection and return to heaven. In Luke 19:10, Jesus gave a glimpse into His reason for coming to earth. He said, "The Son of Man came to seek and save the lost." As He neared the end of His visible time with the apostles, Jesus had to impress upon them the absolute urgency of reaching out to those who had not heard of the offer of salvation through His death, burial, and resurrection.

Therefore the words "shock the wheat" convey an urgent message. If wheat is not harvested when it is ripe the harvest can be lost. My dad's words take on heavenly significance when viewed in light of the truth behind Jeremiah 1:4–7. Here is the account of God calling Jeremiah to be a prophet. Jeremiah objected because of his youth and inexperience. However, God said, "Before I formed you in the womb I knew you, before you were born I set you apart; I appointed you as a prophet to the nations" (Jeremiah 1:5). God knew Jeremiah before he lived in his mother's body. God would not send a spirit He knows to just anyone. The passage in Jeremiah clearly teaches that God knows the spirit of every unborn baby. This means that He selects the parents who will help a God-given child become what God planned in eternity.

When we link the birth story of Jesus with the Jeremiah text and note the way God selected Mary and Joseph, it becomes difficult to doubt that God knows an unborn child and selects his or her human parents. Therefore childbirth is not an accident of nature, but a part of God's wonderful creation. There is no more thrilling fact than the birth of the Lord Jesus. Have you thought about this? How could a birth in a disputed place change the world's calendar, create hospitals and schools, promote care for the downtrodden, inspire courage, and greater still, give peace to rebellious souls while creating loving servants?

The extraordinary birth of Jesus should surprise and thrill us. He was born to poor parents, praised by shepherds, exalted by magi, and believed on by countless millions. We need to see that God acts in ways that we never expect, in places and people we probably would not choose. But this is the way of God.

My dad's words "shock the wheat" speak to the urgent nature of harvesting grain. When grain is ripe it must be cared for or lost. The Gospels refer to "harvest" in Matthew 9:37–38, in Luke 10:2, and in John 4:35. In each of these ministering moments, Jesus focused on the spiritual needs of people and compared His mission on earth to a harvest! A harvest is not about the work involved, but about gathering the crop. I go back to what Dad taught me that day in the wheat field. What mattered was not the weather, the insects, or my physical discomfort. The only thing that mattered was harvesting the wheat.

The apostle Paul certainly grasped the importance of staying focused on the main purpose of his Christ-given ministry. Paul listed numerous possible hindrances to his missionary ministry. He wrote of beatings, hunger, shipwreck, rejections, and betrayals, but there was never a hint of him turning aside for an easier ministry. (See 2 Corinthians 11:16–33.) Paul did not allow anything to keep him from taking the gospel to the lost.

Matthew records that when Jesus saw the crowds of people who followed Him, He was moved with compassion for them. Viewing the many afflictions of the multitude, Jesus said, "The harvest is plentiful" (Matthew 9:37). The harvest was a hurting group of people. Some were sick while others were like neglected sheep. Jesus' concern was for what might today be termed pastoral care. He was saying that one way to reach people with the message of God's love, leading to the salvation of their souls, is to minister to their deep human hurts. Remember that Jesus said, "I am the Good Shepherd" (John 10:11). Who can forget His parable of the lost sheep, which He applied to two situations? In the first, He showed the value God places on children (Matthew 14:10–14). He also applied the principle of ninety-nine to one to "tax collectors and sinners" (Luke 15:1–7).

The Lord was showing that from the very least and weakest to those thought of as the worst sinners and most separated from Him, God amazingly loves them one and all. God does not love us because of what we are, but because of who we are. Who are we? We are people to whom God gave human life and for whom Christ Jesus died. Wonder of wonders, He loves us all!

Luke points to an outreach type of harvest. In Luke 10:1–20, Jesus instructed His disciples to go out and find people in need of spiritual help, even though they might be unaware of their needs. The disciples were to help the sick and to share the good news that the kingdom of God was at hand. Jesus assured His disciples that they were doing God's work, that His power and presence would be with them, and that the way their message was received showed how close people were to God.

The disciples went on their mission in the power of God and returned filled with the joy of the Holy Spirit. The joy that filled the disciples was a fulfillment of another of God's precious promises. "He, who goes out weeping, carrying seed to sow, will return with songs of joy, carrying sheaves with him" (Psalm 126:6).

All too often we who minister see ourselves as failures when our efforts are not received warmly. But our main concern should be whether we faithfully give God's message. Our primary task as believers is to follow God's leadership, leaving the results of our efforts in His hands. We do well to remember God's promise in Isaiah. God told Isaiah, "You do not think like I do, since My thoughts cover more than just the moment. Rain and snow water the earth, and these cause the trees to bud and the grass to grow.

The same thing is true of My Word. It will accomplish My desire in people's lives" (Isaiah 55:8–11, author's paraphrase).

Chapter 4 of John's gospel focuses on the spiritual needs of people who were unacceptable to the Jews. John 4:4 says Jesus had to go through Samaria, but this wasn't so. He could have crossed over the Jordan River and gone around Samaria. Many travelers in those days chose to avoid Samaria, because of the hatred between the Samaritans and the Jews. Jesus decided to return to Galilee through Samaria because it was appointed for Him to minister to a woman at a well.

This divine drama was not an accident. The woman went to the well at the exact moment when Jesus was alone and resting. In requesting a drink, He crossed a cultural divide so that He could minister to a social outcast. The woman answered His simple question with another question: "You are a Jew … how can you ask me for a drink?" (John 4:7–9). Jesus moved the conversation from the physical world into the spiritual realm. He revealed that He can give more than water from Jacob's well. The Lord brought to light the dark secrets of the woman's heart and showed the essence of true worship. This worship is led by the Holy Spirit, and where it takes place does not matter. One can worship at home, while driving, in bed, or at work, because true worship is as Jesus told the woman at the well.

True worshippers will worship the Father in spirit and in truth, for these are the kind of worshippers the Father seeks. (See John 4:5–23.) The woman did what all believers ought to do. She witnessed about the Lord, and a town came to listen to His teaching (John 4:28–42).

Many churches are divided and, in some cases, misguided. I was being shown around a new church community to which I had been called as pastor. As we drove past a small village just outside of town, I asked, "What about those people?" I was told, "That is a low class of people. We do not want them in our church." I knew that day I was headed for trouble. Jesus had problems with a group of people who saw themselves as God's favorites to the exclusion of everyone else. Jesus resisted every attitude that cut off some groups from God and divided people over cultural hang-ups. I am certain He is not pleased with some of the attitudes in His church today.

We, the people of God, seem to have lost our focus on the urgency of the harvest. Human time on earth is so short, and the harvest is so great that we cannot expect to fulfill God's purpose for us unless we "Throw off everything that hinders and the sin that so easily entangles, and … run with perseverance the race marked out for us" (Hebrews 12:1). Therefore, as Jesus said, "Open your eyes and look at the fields! They are ripe for harvest" (John 4:35).

God chose to reveal His Son to us when we were cut off from Him because of our sin. His marvelous grace has touched us with the power of the gospel. We who believe in Christ Jesus the Lord have been touched by the Holy Spirit and have become children of God. Glory! Hallelujah! How can we rest, knowing that the Lord Jesus went to the cross for us and has, by His blood, brought us into the family of God? As God's children, have we forgotten Jesus' word to His disciples? He promised the power of the Holy Spirit to make their witness effective and proclaimed the world their harvest field (Acts 1:8).

Romans 10:13–17 is a most compelling block of Scripture. Look at it! Romans 10:13 is one of God's promises that countless thousands of us have believed and received God's forgiveness by invoking, thereby entering the family of God.

Romans 10:14, however, is a troubling verse. Just as someone told us the gospel story, that same story must be told to those who have not yet asked Jesus to save them.

Shock the Wheat is about God's call to His followers to tell the good news. God gives His people blessings, and when believers walk with Him, He grows them in His grace so they may tell what the Lord has done in their lives.

There can be no clearer example than the demon-possessed man in the region of the Gerasenes whom Jesus delivered from his affliction. Jesus told the man, "Go home to your family and tell them how much the Lord has done for you" (Mark 5:19). The man went throughout the region recounting what Jesus had done for him (Mark 5:20). Surely if a person with his background could give an effective witness for the Lord, we, with all of our technological advances, could do as much.

Take a drive on a busy workday and note the number of people you see. Tune the TV to a football or basketball game and see thousands of people, many of whom quite likely do not know Jesus as Savior and Lord. The world is filling up with people, the harvest is becoming greater, and we are in danger of losing it.

If the fields were white unto harvest in Jesus' day, they are way overripe in our time. The question is, what will we do with our time on earth as Jesus' redeemed people? Will we ignore the harvest needs, or by His grace and power, will we get involved in the harvest of souls for Christ? Let's give ourselves to Jesus and ask Him to make us harvest laborers who are about the task of shocking the Lord's wheat. The harvest waits!

Heavenly Father, help us to grow in our appreciation of Your grace and loving patience. Fill us with a powerful boldness and a godly compassion for everyone who is outside the family of God. Make us, by Your grace, eager harvesters with You. Amen!

CHAPTER 2

A VISIBLE DESTINY

All the days ordained for me were written in your
book before one of them came to be.

—Psalm 139:16

. . . .

In the 1940s, our community always got together at Fairview
Cemetery to celebrate Memorial Day. This Memorial Day was
for me quite significant because God taught me the first of many
truths that in time changed my life. Then as now, it was my habit to
read the names and the dates on tombstones. I wanted to know when
people were born and when they died. I worked my way through
the tombstones and finished on the little knoll where my ancestral
family was buried.

Looking out over the crowd of people, I could see my dad and
my grandfather. Then my gaze fell on my great-great-grandfather
Delaney's gravestone. He was born in 1815. Next to his grave, my
great-grandfather, John James, was buried; he was born in 1852. I am

sitting on my granddad's gravestone, which he had set up to mark his final resting place, and he was born in 1876.

Delaney was the oldest; he had died and there was his grave. John James, Delaney's son, had died and was buried next to his father. George Laney, John James's son, was still alive, but one day he would be buried where I sat. My dad, William Henry, George Laney's son, had not chosen his spot, but one day he would die and be buried on this hillside. Cemeteries speak to the basic nature of the human race. Take a walk in a cemetery and it will teach you that some die young and some die old, but everyone dies.

I realized that one day I would die and the next day the sun would come up in the same place as before. My first understanding of life on earth was that it would end in death. The Bible says in Isaiah 40:6–7 and 1 Peter 1:24–25 that all people are like grass. Think about it. Our bodies have no more eternal longevity than a blade of grass. We may live longer, but in the end our human flesh returns to dust just like grass.

However, God has more in store for us than to finish our days on earth in a cemetery. He created us flesh and spirit. This earth will hold the dust of our physical existence, but the spiritual part of us will never die because God has planned and provided another place of residence for every human spirit. The choice of where is one each of us must make.

Cemeteries also call to mind times of sadness. The death of a loved one brings us grief. People who are grieving need loving care. In 1945 my dad's sister Naomi died from a devastating sexual disease that shortened many lives. Aunt Naomi, at the end of her life, was placed in a Louisville hospital where she passed away. Her body was shipped home on a train, and she was laid out for viewing in our home.

Naomi's relatives gathered and made funeral plans. They soon discovered a problem. No preacher in the community would conduct Naomi's funeral. There were several reasons, I suspect. Some may not have had time; others may have been afraid that doing so would spoil their reputation. I do not know for sure, but I do know this. My family had no church home, and apparently no one had a preacher friend. I can still hear the anguished sobbing of Naomi's sister as she cried out, "No one will preach her funeral."

Someone said, "There is a new Baptist preacher in Berea. Maybe he will do it for us." Later my aunt told this story. "We sat in Reverend O. B. Mylum's office," she recalled, "and I asked him to preach Naomi's funeral, and he immediately said yes." My aunt said, "I need to tell you about her life and our situation." Reverend Mylum's said, "No. That is not necessary." My aunt insisted and told her story to the minister. Pastor Mylum leaned over his desk, patted her on the shoulder, and said, "Honey, it's okay; I will do it for you." And he did!

I have no memory of anything O. B. Mylum said, only what he did at Aunt Naomi's funeral. The loving care he gave my family during our time of grief touched my young heart. Sadly, he never knew that I did my best to imitate his compassion in every grief situation I encountered. I never refused to preach a funeral. I can only say thank God for men like O. B. Mylum who pattern their lives after Jesus.

Sometimes we get caught up in the awesome truth of God's Word about life beyond the grave, and heaven seems more real than earth. At such times we whisper with Paul, "For to me, to live is

Christ and to die is gain … yet what shall I chose? I do not know! I am torn between the two: I desire to depart and be with Christ which is better by far; but it is more necessary for you that I remain" (Philippians 1:21, 23–24). When we know Jesus as Savior and Lord, as the old hymn says, "This world is not our home. We are just passing through."

As I grow older and have seen dear friends and loved ones pass on to the next life, my heart longs to see them. However, that will happen in God's appointed time. I think of the many women and men left alone by the passing of a lifetime partner. These hurting people are wrapped in a veil of loneliness, worn like a cloak that hides their aching hearts. Only those who have experienced such heart-wrenching, breathtaking loss can appreciate the value of the words of James, the brother of the Lord. He wrote, "Religion that God our Father accepts as pure and faultless is this: To look after orphans and widows in their distress" (James 1:27).

A born-again believer in Christ need not fear death. We do, however, need to accept the fact that in God's time death comes to everyone. Most of the people I have been with who were nearing death wanted to get their lives right with God. The psalmist put it this way: "I long to … take refuge in the shelter of your wings" (Psalm 61:4). Believers in Christ know that He has sheltered them from the sting of death by His death on the cross. "Death has been swallowed up in victory … through our Lord Jesus Christ" (1 Corinthians 15:54, 57).

Believers can pass into eternity without fear, knowing full well that Jesus is waiting with open arms. I saw firsthand such faith for living and dying when my first wife, Beth, went to meet the Lord. We knew for seventeen days that she had terminal liver cancer. Not once in those days did Beth show fear or anxiety. The entire family drew strength from her. In fact, she spent her last days planning my future. She instructed me to eat properly, to take my shirts to the laundry, and not to look like a sloppy old man. She also knew I would not be happy living alone and made me promise to pray much about whomever I decided to marry. I can say with all assurance that many years before her death, Beth had moved from the shadow of death into the shelter of the cross of Christ.

Dr. Donald Grey Barnhouse told this story following the funeral of his first wife. He and his three children were on their way home from the funeral service. The children were naturally overcome with grief. Barnhouse said he was trying to think of some way to comfort them. Just then a large moving van passed them and cast its shadow over them. As the truck moved on, Barnhouse said an inspiration came to him. "Children," he asked, "would you rather be run over by a truck or by its shadow?" The children said, "Well, of course the shadow, Dad. The truck would hurt but the shadow cannot hurt us." Barnhouse said, "Did you know that two thousand years ago the truck of death ran over the Lord Jesus so that only the shadow of death might run over us?" [1]

We can live by Jesus' words, and we can die knowing He will keep His promise to us. Even as I write these words and you read them, Jesus is preparing a place for all of God's children. In God's appointed time, when everything is made ready, He will come and usher us into our heavenly home. Are you living in the shadow of death or under the shelter of Christ's cross? Think for a moment

1   Michael P. Green, ed., *Illustrations for Biblical Preaching* p-91 (Baker Book House, 1999)

about the horizontal beam of Jesus' cross. His arms stretched out on the cross beam can easily be pictured as wings under which we are sheltered from the shadow of death. Jesus has rescued us from the shadow of death and delivered us into the sheltering grace of God's kingdom. Hallelujah!

A shelter is a place of refuge during a storm. A friend and I were golfing and about to make the turn toward the clubhouse when the rain came in sheets parallel to the ground. Thankfully, management had built a shelter to protect golfers in this situation. Storms of various kinds continually roll across the landscape of our lives. The question is, where do we go during these storms? Hopefully, we follow the writer of Proverbs, who said, "The Lord is my rock, my fortress, and my deliverer in whom I take refuge" (Proverbs 30:5).

However, a shelter becomes a refuge only when we exercise faith and accept its protection. The Old Testament offers many examples of how God sheltered His people, and each one hinged on believing Him. God's sheltering care of His people is sometimes described as a shield, as protection, as a haven of safety, and as deliverance and defense. God told Abraham, "I am your shield" (Genesis 15:1). God promised to be Abraham's protection in a hostile land. Abraham "believed the Lord, and He credited to Abraham righteousness" (Genesis 15:6). David sang of God's care for him, saying, "The Lord is my ... deliverer ... He is my shield ... my stronghold" (Psalm 18:2). According to Scripture, God sheltered, shielded, provided a haven of safety, and delivered from danger countless times when His people obeyed His Word and rested in His promise. As John H. Yates' hymn says, "Faith is the victory, we know, that overcomes the world."

When the people of God demonstrate faith in His protection, their faith moves God to action. Consider this definition of faith. "Now faith is being sure of what we hope for and certain of what we do not see" (Hebrews 11:1).

The belief that God shelters His people grew to include the faith that He was also in control of human life beyond physical death. The psalmist says, "The eyes of the Lord are on those who fear Him, on those whose hope is in His unfailing love to deliver them from death" (Psalm 33:18). Granted the writer may be praying about his daily concern for safety. However, the idea of deliverance from death advanced the notion about God's place in life after death.

The question, then, is whether the Lord is God not only of the living but also of those who have died. Jesus clearly says that God is God of the living and also of all who believed in Jesus' work of salvation even though they have died to the flesh. The Lord asked, "Have you not read what God said to you, I am the God of Abraham, the God of Isaac, and the God of Jacob? He is not the God of the dead but of the living" (Matthew 22:31–32). If God is the God of those who have died physically and of the living, then those who served God are still living.

The apostle Paul, dealing with the lack of faith in life beyond the grave, said, "If only for this life we have hope in Christ, we are to be pitied more than all men" (1 Corinthians 15:19). When we belong to Christ, physical death is not the end of our existence. Death for a believer is but the vehicle that opens the door to eternal life in the Spirit. Jesus promised to prepare a place for us and to come and take us there when everything was ready (John 14:14). He is the God of the living, and believers in Jesus' death, burial, and resurrection will not die spiritually but will live with God in His eternity.

The writer of Hebrews, speaking to second-generation believers and seeking to encourage them, pointed to the faithfulness of God. The writer, whoever he was, possessed a living hope that Jesus cared for believers whether on earth or in heaven. He began with the fact that Abraham received what God promised him, because "It is impossible for God to lie" (Hebrews 6:18). Therefore, "We who have fled to take hold of the hope offered us may be greatly encouraged" (Hebrews 6:18). We can be encouraged by the faithfulness of God to do what He says.

Furthermore, we can come to Jesus, who is seated at the right hand of God, and receive His help now and in the hereafter. The writer continued his encouragement by pointing out that "Jesus went before us, and has entered [the inner sanctuary behind the curtain] on our behalf. He has become a high priest forever" (Hebrews 6:20).

As our High Priest in the inner sanctuary of God's holy heaven, Jesus continues His loving care of His people. While we remain on earth and face the daily struggles of temptation and sin, "we have one who speaks to the Father in our defense—Jesus Christ the righteous one" (1 John 2:1). Also, since Jesus is alive in heaven, "He is able to save completely those who come to God through Him, because He always lives to intercede for them" (Hebrews 7:25).

May the grace of God flood our hearts with the love of Christ and give us light to see the wonder of His sheltering grace—the marvelous gift that teaches God's peace, reveals the glory of His presence, and comforts us in trying times. Lord, increase our faith! Amen.

CHAPTER 3

LIFE BEYOND THE VISIBLE

You will know the truth, and the truth will set you free.

— John 8:32

· ·

There is an existence beyond what we can see with human eyes. This invisible reality, the kingdom of God, can be reached only by faith in the love of God. Belief in God can lead to a level of faith that will open the door of eternity and usher us into the eternal life of God in Christ.

My most important childhood lesson came on a winter day when snow and ice covered the ground. Our family attended church, and the pastor preached from the third chapter of John. The pastor was a veteran of World War I and had been exposed to poison gas in the trenches of France. The gas affected his vocal cords and left him with a speech problem. However, the message came through as he repeated over and over, "You must be born again" (John 3:3). I heard the preacher, but I had no clue what the words meant except that somehow something had to happen to my heart or I would go to hell.

Three unavoidable truths demand our attention when we consider that Jesus said to Nicodemus, "I tell you the truth, no one can see the kingdom of God unless he is born again" (John 3:3). The third chapter of John is Jesus' three *M* sermon. The three *Ms* of salvation are the must, the mystery, and the master of all salvation experiences.

In John 3:3 Jesus told Nicodemus the way to get into heaven. He said that a new birth is a must for entry. Every person was physically born into the world. A physical birth is necessary to be a human being. Faced with Jesus' absolute condition for entrance into heaven, thinking people know that something must happen to them and that they cannot do it themselves. Just as we humans cannot cause ourselves to be born into this world, neither can we birth ourselves into God's holy heaven.

We humans in our natural state cannot get into heaven. It is a spiritual place for which.our fleshly bodies were not made. They were created solely for earthly existence. The problem is that sin has corrupted us, and to get into heaven our personal sin must somehow be taken away. Jesus showed clearly that we are both flesh and spirit when He said, "Flesh gives birth to flesh, but the Spirit [that is the Holy Spirit of God] gives birth to Spirit" (John 3:6). Since flesh and blood cannot enter heaven, it is our spirit that must be changed.

The second great truth concerning the new-birth experience is that it is enveloped in a great mystery. Hearing Nicodemus's question comparing being born again to physical birth, Jesus told him, "You should not be surprised at my saying, you must be born again. The wind blows wherever it pleases. You hear its sound, but you cannot tell where it comes from or where it is going. So it is with everyone born of the Spirit" (John 3:7–8).

That trees bend in the wind is itself a mystery. We cannot see the wind, only its effects. We believe by faith that there is such a thing as wind, because we see the results. The same holds true for the Holy Spirit of God. We cannot see Him, but we can harness His power simply by believing in His willingness to do for us what He did for Jesus when He brought Him from the tomb alive. Paul pointed to the Holy Spirit's ability to work in human life when he spoke of God's "incomparable great power for us who believe. That power is like the working of His mighty strength, which He exerted in Christ when he raised him from the dead" (Ephesians 1:19–20).

The third and most wonderful truth concerning the new birth is that Jesus is the master of this experience. Reminding Nicodemus of a well-known event in Jewish history, the Lord said, "Just as Moses lifted up the snake in the desert, so the Son of Man must be lifted up, that everyone who believes in Him may have eternal life" (John 3:14–15). While the children of Israel wandered in the wilderness, they got into trouble with God. To punish them, He sent an epidemic of poisonous snakes among them, and many Israelites died. God's plan of deliverance was unique. He told Moses, "'Make a snake and put it on a pole; anyone who is bitten can look at it and live' … When anyone was bitten by a snake and looked at the bronze snake, he lived" (Numbers 21:8–9).

Those without faith in God's mighty power will probably question this story. Some say there is no way that looking at an object can affect deadly venom racing through one's body. They are correct—unless

God caused something beyond human ability to happen, which is exactly what occurred, because the Israelites survived.

Take a leap of faith, and see Jesus hanging on the cross. He was there dying for the sins of all mankind. Jesus said that everyone who believes in Him will have eternal life (John 3:15). God can fix sin, and sin is fixed when we confess it and believe Jesus died for our transgressions. Only then are we born new in the spirit. The new birth brings us into God's spiritual family and makes us His children. Jesus set the standard we had to reach to get into heaven, and He also paid our admission price. Therefore we can spend eternity with God. Hallelujah!

What I heard on that cold winter morning left me with the knowledge that if I were to die, I would go to hell. Paul says in Romans, "Everyone who calls on the name of the Lord will be saved. How, then, can they call on the one they have not believed in? How can they believe in the one of whom they have not heard? And how can they hear without someone preaching to them?" (Romans 10:13–14). Herein lies a problem. People may realize they are cut off from God but never know what to do about it. Unless someone gives them the message of God's love and offer of forgiveness, they have little hope of ever becoming part of God's holy family.

There are two unavoidable truths about life. Number one, death is certain. No one gets out of this world alive. Second, heaven is real, and everyone who believes in Jesus' death, burial, and resurrection can go there.

So far as I remember, no one told me about Jesus dying on a cross for my sin until I was about fifteen years old. Here is how I heard. Dad operated a saw mill, and during the noon hour, a preacher drove up and asked for a load of sawdust. He was holding a tent revival and needed sawdust to cover the ground. I loaded the preacher's truck, and he invited us to attend the revival services.

A Methodist layman owned a junk yard and moved the wrecked cars to make room for the revival tent. A Salvation Army preacher brought the sermon, and during one of the services that my family and I attended, he told of Jesus' death on the cross for the forgiveness of sin. This was the first time I remember hearing of Jesus dying on a cross. A light came on in my mind, because now I knew what to do about the prospect of hell. During the next month or so, I wrestled in my mind with how someone who had been on earth hundreds of years before could die for my sins. Eventually, God gave me the faith to believe Jesus could do what the preacher said He could do.

God began to deal with me. I knew there were some things I would have to quit doing. God was teaching me about repentance, and I felt I had to give up five habitual sins. They were not big sins, since I was only fifteen. I tried to bargain with God. I asked, "Can I give up one, three, and five and keep two and four?" I knew the answer was no. All of them had to go. Finally, as the Holy Spirit worked in my heart, I came to the place where I said, "Okay, I will stop all these things, but how do you save me?"

I knew that Jesus had died for my sins and that He would forgive them. I also knew that I had to turn from my sins for Him to save me. My question became, "How can You save me and give me a new life?" God's simple answer was, "Trust me." Oh yeah! The problem was that I had little trust in anyone or anything. For days I was hung up on how to trust.

The answer came in a strange way. I had read a book centered on a castle. The villains continually foiled the hero. He could never corner them. Finally he discovered that behind the castle walls was a deep chasm with a ledge on each side. The bad guys would swing across the chasm on ropes to escape the hero. In my mind Jesus brought me to the edge of this black chasm. I could see my toes hanging over the edge, and He seemed to be saying, "Just trust me. Step off and I will catch you." Was God for real and could He be trusted? Would He really forgive my sins and make my heart new? That's what I had to decide.

One night, by faith, I stepped into the unknown darkness and found Jesus waiting with open arms. He forgave my sin, brought me into His kingdom, and welcomed me as a child of God.

At this point in my Christian life, the words of Winston Churchill were applicable. England had achieved a small victory against Germany. Asked if this victory had turned the tide in the war, Churchill said, "This is not the end of the fight; it is only the end of the beginning." History shows that victory came following a long struggle. So it is with the Christian life. Tragically, many born-again believers never grow beyond their initial experience with the Lord.

It grieves me to say that my early life in Christ was what I call my "Adam experience." That is, I hid from God. He was always seeking me, but I kept Him at a distance. I was God's own; He had bought me with the price of His Son's death, but the "much more" Paul speaks of in Romans 5 was not part of my life. Romans 10:9–10 makes clear that to become all God wants us to be, Jesus must be both our Savior and Lord. The name Jesus means that He is the Savior. When the angel announced to Joseph that Mary would give birth to a son, he said, "You are to give him the name Jesus, because he will save his people from their sins" (Matthew 1:21). Jesus is the Savior because he died for the sins of everyone. Lord means that to please Him, to serve Him, and to receive His blessing. He must be in charge of our lives. Simply said, He is the boss or ruler of all aspects of a believer's life.

To be true servants of Christ, we must revere Jesus as both Savior and Lord. I received Jesus as Savior more than sixty-five years ago. Unfortunately, He did not immediately become Lord of my life. Even so, He never left me, but continued to place situations and people in my life to turn my heart to Him.

Soon after my conversion I knew in my heart that God was calling me to be a preacher. Had I been asked to explain how I knew that God wanted me to be a preacher, I could not have given a clear answer. The best explanation may be that when Jesus saves us and takes up residence in our souls, He can communicate His will without making a sound. One need not wonder or doubt if God is calling. He will make His will known beyond all question.

I never shared my feeling of being called to preach with anyone, and I told God, "I am not going to do that!" I knew nothing about church, and preachers were not high on my list of favorite people. However, I would eventually understand that God did not take my rebellion seriously. In the early days of my Christian life, I saw God as an authority figure like my dad. Therefore I felt that if I ignored him long enough He would forget. God's awesome power and the eternal nature of Christ's work on the cross were foreign to me.

I would learn that the blood of Jesus had bought me and that, as a child of God, I was in His family for good. When Christ enters our lives He is there to stay. "We are not our own. We have been bought with the price of the life of Jesus" (1 Corinthians 6:20). Since we belong to Jesus, nothing and no one can remove God from our lives. This lesson came slowly over the next few years.

Paul wrote, "If anyone is in Christ, he is a new creation; the old has gone, the new has come" (2 Corinthians 5:17). A person born physically cannot be unborn, any more than a word spoken can be unspoken. So also in the spirit realm with God, a spirit born anew in the divine image cannot be unborn. When we give our hearts to Jesus and become children of God, we will never cease to be His children. Following my salvation experience, I entered the United States Air Force, and for some time I did nothing that would have convinced anyone that I had been saved. However, I would come to understand that I felt empty and lacked a purpose in life because I was continually grieving the Holy Spirit. Little wonder that I was constantly searching for more and for a reason to live.

I received my discharge from the Air Force near the end of the Korean War. A high school classmate had been killed in combat, and his body was brought home for burial. I was a pallbearer at his funeral. Sometime later I meet my friend's grieving brother, who asked, "Why did my brother die and you live?" I did not respond, because I did not know why I was still alive or why a person whom I held in high regard had been killed.

I sincerely wondered, *why am I alive?* God has a process that leads to the discovery of why a believer in Christ has eternal life. Someone asked John Henry Jowett, a preacher of another century, why Jesus chose Judas. Jowett said, "I have a harder question than that. Why did God choose me?" I suspect that most of us, when we are humbly honest, understand what Jowett meant. However, God did choose us, and by His grace overlooked our past and nailed it to the cross of Jesus. Therefore the way we were does not limit God's plan for our lives in Christ. Writing about a believer's new life in Christ, Paul said, "We are God's workmanship, created in Christ Jesus to do good works, which God prepared in advance for us to do" (Ephesians 2:10).

Heavenly Father, I thank You for thinking of us. We humbly believe in Your call to salvation and service. Please help us grow to Your higher purpose so we can live in such a way that those around us see Jesus. Fill us with Your Spirit so that whatever You need us to do, be it word or deed, You will find us ready. Amen!

CHAPTER 4

THE ONE AND ONLY

Surely the Lord is in this place, and I was not aware of it.

— Genesis 28:16

. . . .

Does God have specific places where He wants His people to live? Yes! Has God chosen the people He wants His children to know, love, and marry? Yes! Are we then just puppets struggling at the end of God's manipulative string? No! Clearly we have a free will to pick the course in life we desire. However, God is also free to manage the circumstances of our lives. This world and time as we know it belong to God. He makes all things work so that we have the freedom to arrive at the place He desires on time.

As I consider my early Christian years, I can pinpoint many times when God clearly influenced the outcome of life-changing events. When I finished basic training at Lackland Air Force Base in San Antonio, Texas, I was sent to Scott Air Force Base in Belleville, Illinois, to study radio mechanics.

During the winter months we were given several three-day weekends. About the same time there was an outbreak of measles, which I did not catch until I went home on a three-day pass. The doctor and the Red Cross notified the base, and I was not counted absent without leave. However, I missed a week of class and was put back with the next class.

In June of 1950, the Korean War broke out, and when my original class graduated members were shipped to Camp Stoneman, California, for assignment overseas. The following week, I also received orders to go to Stoneman for overseas assignment. I cleared the base and needed only my First Sergeant's approval to leave.

However, when I reached the squadron I was told to have a seat and wait for further orders. My original orders had been changed from Camp Stoneman to Randolph Air Force Base in San Antonio, Texas. This may seem of little importance except that from Randolph I went to Bryan Air Force Base in Bryan, Texas. In Bryan, I began to search for the meaning of life, and it was there that I met, fell in love with, and married Laura Beth Meads, on November 26, 1952. I know this was God's special plan for my life. Beth was the person God had chosen to help change my direction and to clarify His purpose for my life. She was a vital part of my life and my ministry for more than fifty-five years.

I stress this point because it is vital to understand that God often directs our lives through circumstances outside of our control. I confess that I never thought God was the least bit involved in the events in my life, events that brought me to Bryan Air Force Base. However, had it not been for the measles, for the fifteen minutes in which my orders were changed, and for a glance at a bulletin board that showed an opening at Bryan Air Force Base, I never would have met Beth. If God had not worked through Beth, I seriously doubt I would have been of much use to the Lord Jesus. Yes, I believe that the people God providentially brings into our lives are vital to His plan for us.

For several years I worked at a paper mill. I had begun to attend church with Beth, and services were becoming a part of my life. One day at the mill, the temperature was almost unbearable and the paper kept breaking. The floor was knee deep in scrap paper. I began to curse the heat, the paper mill, and the problems we were having. Profanity was my native tongue. I was the oldest grandchild and my elders taught me to curse early. They thought it was cute! Profanity became easy and was my first choice in stressful situations. However, in the midst of my cursing spasm, I suddenly realized what I was doing, and for the first time in my life I felt guilt. I whispered a prayer, saying, "Please, God, help me never to do this kind of thing again." At that moment, profanity ceased to be my spontaneous language. The lesson is clear. In His time, God convicts a person for a sinful attitude or a moral evil; He will also give the help needed to make a change.

I have heard it said that the excessive use of profanity shows a lack of intelligence. I am not so sure about this because I have known people who could string together profanity in such a creative way that they surely had high verbal skills. Dr. Wayne Oats, pastoral care professor at Southern Seminary, says that profanity points to a lack of relationship with God. He is right!

A friend whom I knew from childhood was uneducated and did not speak one sentence without using profanity. He had managed to get together enough money to buy a few heifers and then bought himself a bull. He knocked on my door one morning and asked if I could go with him to look at his bull, which was unable to get up. The animal was infected with shipping fever and very near death. My friend asked, "What do you think?" I replied, "It does not look like he will make it."

This dear man began to beat his leg with his hat and to curse. As I watched him I thought, *if I were in his shoes I would be praying.* But tragically all he could do to express his deep hurt and great need was to curse. I am convinced that Oats was correct. When a person's dreams are crashing and the anguished soul cries out in profanity, the only cure is to know the deep abiding love of Christ the Lord. At moments like this, as Paul says, "In Him [Christ] and through faith in Him we may approach God with freedom and confidence" (Ephesians 3:12). Only God knows how many times, in the wrenching crises of life, I have sought and received the loving, comforting help of God the Father. We are never alone when Christ is our Lord and Savior.

Working in the paper mill was like marching in place. I was doing something but getting nowhere. A man nearing retirement told me, "I have been here in this building for thirty-five years and have loved every minute of it." I thought, *I could never do that.* For me, there was no purpose for being there beyond the paycheck. The need for a meaningful reason to be alive is a God-created force that drives us to seek inner peace, even though we may be unable to explain this unrelenting quest. God created us to walk and to talk with Him, and without Him in our lives we are like roadside scavengers feeding on scraps. We fill our lives with unsatisfying things and relationships, trying without success to fill an emptiness in our souls that only God can fill.

This empty feeling prompts us to ask, "Why am I alive?" The reason for life will remain a mystery until we get to where God has in place a system to grow us toward spiritual maturity. In my search for meaning, I have discovered that why is not the first and most important question in seeking to know the reason for our existence. In fact, we may never know why we are alive unless we connect with the people and events that God has prepared to shape our lives. The apostle Paul preached to the men of Athens that God not only created them from one man, Adam, but also "determined the times for them and the exact places where they should live" (Acts 17:26).

Where you are spiritually and geographically seems to matter to God. That is to say, what is the desire of your heart, and where are you seeking to fulfill that desire? When you are in the geographical place God intends for you, He uses people and life situations to fuel the desire of your heart. I could not know why I was alive until I was in the place where God wanted me to be. And before I could know the why of my life, I needed to know who I was in Christ Jesus. We need to know that God made us His children and that He has a purpose in mind for each of us.

Why are we alive and children of God? We are alive to bring glory to God. We glorify God when we join Him in working to grow His kingdom on earth. That is the why of every born-again believer. We have the God-given ability to carry out a life of service to the Father by the fullness of His Holy Spirit. God gives us His Spirit to teach us how to overcome temptation and to serve Him in such a way that He is glorified. Knowing who we are, why we are, and how we can glorify God brings us back to His ordained where.

This was certainly true in the life of Joseph. God's appointed place for him was Egypt, where he learned who he was, why he was, and how he could carry out God's plan for his life. (See Genesis 37–46.)

God's where is discovered by going through the door He opens. God has planned a certain spot on the planet where He has His servants in place to grow us into the people He created us to be.

My relationship with God began at conversion, but I did nothing to mature the experience. Even so, God was there all the time. He was working behind the scenes, waiting for me to call on Him. Though I didn't realize it, I was searching for more of God in my life. We who believe in Jesus should remember that He placed no conditions on His promise when He said, "I am with you always" (Matthew 28:20).

The Holy Spirit of Christ is always present in a believer's life, even though sin may force Him into the shadows. He is always there, waiting patiently for that sure-to-happen teachable moment. The Holy Spirit is with us because, as Paul says, "Your body is a temple of the Holy Spirit, who is in you, whom you have received from God" (1 Corinthians 6:19). Since we are living temples where God dwells, He goes where we go and we never leave home without Him.

How does faith grow to where we are certain God is always present? God told Abraham to look up and see Him at work in the universe. The stars are too many to count and point to the awesome greatness of almighty God (Genesis 15:5–6). The apostle

Paul picked up on this idea and went so far as to say that God holds us accountable for how we receive His revelation in creation (Romans 1:19–20).

Without question, God loves humans and desires to give them His good life. However, God has always had to deal with man's limitations. We humans do not think, act, or feel like God, because sin has polluted our existence. Therefore God must find a way to reveal Himself in every person's life. Remember that Jesus came to earth to show us the unending love of the heavenly Father.

Psalm 19 beautifully presents the process of God's revelation to mankind. His general revelation is in the heavens for all to see. The sky filled with the sun, moon, and stars proclaims that there is a creative hand at work and a power beyond human capacity. Verse 3 says that the silent message of a creative God is seen everywhere on earth. This visible evidence of God as creator makes every person accountable before Him.

This psalm reveals a special message. God is not content to have mankind believe He is the creator of all, but also wants people to act in certain ways toward Him and humanity. Thus God's self-revelation leads to an understanding that He expects His creation to be like Him. In leading people to know Him, God reveals the powerful truth of his Word. God's purpose in His revelation is that His Word will become "more precious than gold ... sweeter than honey" to people (Psalm 19:10).

It has been said that as a man thinks in his heart so is he. God's spiritual revelation moves our hearts. When we believe God's Word, the Holy Spirit urges us to cry out, "May the words of my mouth and the meditations of my heart be pleasing in your sight, O Lord, my Rock and my Redeemer" (Psalm 19:14). Holy Father, do this in me.

The Holy Spirit of God makes the message of the stars real. Often slowly but always gently and firmly, the Holy Spirit makes us aware that we are missing Jesus' plan for our lives (John 16:5–16). Jesus said, "You will know the truth, and the truth will set you free" (John 8:32). He is the truth that sets us free from the lost condition that infects all people. He also said, "Apart from me you can do nothing" (John 15:5). As Peter told the Sanhedrin, "There is no other name under heaven given to men by whom we must be saved" (Acts 4:12). Hallelujah, we are free in Christ to be all God planned when He knew us in eternity and sent our spirits to earth for a short time.

When we accept God as creator of the heavens and believe that He placed every star in all the galaxies in orbit, that the entire universe moves in concert more perfect than the best-designed Olympic routine, that the seasons of spring, fall, summer, and winter arrive in response to the orbit of the galaxies, that cells in our bodies cooperate to keep us healthy, make us sleepy, and give us energy, is it too difficult to believe that God also has a plan for our lives? A plan that not only includes serving Him, but also where and how we are to respond to our creative and loving heavenly Father.

The prophet Elijah discovered that God had a special spot on the planet for him to live at a precise point in time. God had a place where He needed His prophet to be, a place where He would provide for his physical needs, where Elijah's faith in God would grow stronger, and where he would glorify God by helping people.

Elijah burst on the political scene with the suddenness of a tornado on a clear day. Like an eagle swooping down on its unsuspecting prey,

Elijah announced God's message to King Ahab. The prophet said, "There will be neither dew nor rain in the next few years except at my word" (1 Kings 17:1). When the grass stopped growing for lack of rain and the dry ground cracked open, the king put a bounty on Elijah, and I suspect he would have put the screws to the prophet to make him bring rain.

But God was ahead of the game. He had a plan in place to protect the prophet and to provide for his physical needs. God told Elijah, "Leave here … hide in Kerith Ravine … you will drink from the brook, and I have ordered the ravens to feed you there" (1 Kings 17:4). Elijah would eat God's provisions and receive His protection in God's appointed "there." Would God's food and protection be available in any old place? No, only in the place where His care was promised. Given the harshness of the Israeli landscape, living by a brook would most definitely test Elijah's faith.

However, many faithful servants of God live and serve where living conditions are not physically or emotionally comfortable. I wonder how many times Elijah replayed in his mind the word God gave him to speak to King Ahab and the instructions about where to hide out? Do not miss this truth. Elijah had to reach the precise place where God wanted him to be. He also had to be thinking about what God wanted him to do next, because not much was happening near the brook. Perhaps most important, Elijah had to continue believing that he had heard God correctly and that he could not leave until God told him to go. So he stayed by the brook.

No doubt Elijah noticed that the brook was getting lower and lower. I wonder if he ever said, "Lord, we have a problem. The brook is about to go dry." He may have wondered if God would split open a rock and provide water as He had done for Moses and the Israelites in the wilderness. However, he stayed until a new word came from the Lord. Elijah got where God told him to be, and he stayed there until the brook dried up. "Then the word of the Lord came to him: 'Go at once to Zarephath … and stay there. I have commanded a widow in that place to supply you with food.' So he went" (1 Kings 17:9–10).

Elijah had been living by faith in God's promise that a raven would feed him. God's new command was equally unlikely because widows were among the people most likely to be without food in times of depression. The widow was in desperate condition when Elijah asked for a piece of bread. She answered, "I don't have any bread and only a handful of flour in a jar and a little oil … for myself and my son, that we may eat it and die" (1 Kings 17:12). Elijah replied, "Don't be afraid … Make a small cake of bread for me … the God of Israel says, 'The jar of flour will not be used up and the jug of oil will not run dry until the day the Lord gives rain'" (1 Kings 17:13–14).

This was a call to faith. The widow had to believe the man of God, but remember that God had said, "I have commanded a widow in that place to supply you with food." The widow did as the prophet requested, and the flour and oil did not run out. This was faith in action. Elijah had to go to God's appointed place and trust that God would move the heart of the widow to have faith. So in times of trouble the question is, should our focus be on the dwindling supply or on the faithfulness of God? The obvious answer is not to focus on the problem, but on the problem solver. God had a special place to provide for Elijah and a specific person to use in providing for His prophet.

Many of us have experienced dry brooks. Sometimes, because of disobedience or a lack of faith, we so pollute our stream of blessings from God that He will not allow us to use His provisions for sinful pursuits. God also may dry up the brook in your life to get your attention and to move you to His new plan and perhaps another and better brook.

The ravens were only at the Kerith Ravine, and the widow was only at Zarephath. These were exclusive places where God had stored provisions and stationed persons to use in carrying out His will. We who believe in Christ Jesus also need to reach God's special place, because this is where He has the people and the resources to provide for our physical needs and to grow us in Christ's likeness.

Heavenly Father, help us to faithfully remain in Your appointed place. Please teach us to listen for Your voice, and increase our faith to take the first step toward Your special "there" for our lives. Amen!

CHAPTER 5

IT'S NOW OR NEVER

Jesus said, "This happened so that the work of
God might be displayed."

—John 9:3

. . . .

Do accidents, sickness, failures, or defeats mean there is sin in our lives? Judging by Scripture, it seems this was a common question in first-century Judea. However, if God made us sick when we sinned, we would never see a healthy day. It is true that some lifestyles result in physical problems, but we can never know why some people go through life in pain while others seldom suffer. Nor do we know why some die young while others live long lives. But we do know that God can work for our good and His glory in every life situation. In the millisecond between heartbeats, accidents take place, injuries happen, and life is forever changed.

Such was the case when I rammed a piece of steel into my hand. The injury resulted in blood poisoning and required surgery to release the infection. I vividly recall the pastor of the church that Beth and I attended visiting me. He is in heaven now, and I hope he has forgiven my bad manners. The preacher was talking to me and I turned my back on him and looked out the window. This man of God came to bring the Lord's comfort and to offer a prayer for my recovery, and I insulted him. He was a wise man, and perhaps he understood that my rejection of him reflected my sense of guilt and my rejection of God's claim on my life.

The surgery required that I be put to sleep. I was terrified, fearing I would never wake up. The anesthesiologist gave me sodium pentothal, but I did not quickly go to sleep. The doctor asked, "Are you getting sleepy?" I said no. He then asked, "How do you feel?" The doc threw me a curve. He tricked me into thinking about something other than not going to sleep. From that point all I remember is saying, "I feel like my legs are going to bust …"

In that day the medicine of choice was penicillin. The side effects were disastrous for some people. I was released from the hospital on a Friday but had to be carried back on Sunday with a severe reaction to the medicine. I was twenty-five years old and could not get out of bed because the remedy for penicillin reaction was adrenaline, and this made my heart beat too fast.

On Thursday morning in Mercy Hospital in Hamilton, Ohio, time seemed to stand still. The sunlight streamed through the cracks in the window shade. God spoke to my heart and said, "If you are not going to do what I saved you and called you to do, then there is no reason for Me to leave you in this world."

He had my attention. This was a blank-check kind of moment. I whispered in my heart, *I do not know what You want, but from this day forward I will give You a tithe of everything I get.* I have kept that promise, and God has never ceased to give me the wisdom to manage the 90 percent far better than I would have used the 100 percent.

You may be wondering why I promised to give God a tithe when He called me to account. Although I was a born-again child of God, I lived like a pagan. I did not read the Bible, witness, worship, praise, give thanks, or intercede for others. I did none of the things that bring glory to God. On the other hand, I cursed, smoked, lusted after women, and acted selfishly.

When Beth and I were dating, I was in the air force and made less than a hundred dollars a month. She taught me about tithing, and I would give her 10 percent of my income, which she kept, and we would contribute a part of that each week. Tithing was the only one of God's instructions that I had ever obeyed. On this day I did the only thing I knew to do. Looking back, I can see that this is God's way. He takes us where we are and patiently leads us to a place of faith and practice that gives Him glory and us unspeakable joy in His appointed place of service.

Through the years as a pastor, I have watched the spiritual progress of God's people. I am convinced that true discipleship begins with a commitment to give God at least a tithe. When we tithe our income to God, we are putting Him first and the physical world second.

Once a month our crew at the paper mill would have five days off, and Beth and I would go back to Kentucky. For a while, I would write a check for our tithe and leave it at home, but I had begun to keep it in my pocket until the next Sunday. On one trip I passed a vehicle on a yellow line, and a trooper gave me a ticket. I do not believe in accidents when it comes to God's discipline. I paid a fine in the exact amount of my tithe. God was teaching me that His tithe belonged in His church, not in my pocket. Furthermore, I was developing a careless habit of taking lightly God's claim on His tithe.

Our church was promoting its annual budget, and the committee challenged us to pledge a set amount for the New Year. Beth and I prayed over it and decided to make the commitment. Little did we know that I would surrender to the ministry, change jobs, and be out of work at the end of the year. The last Sunday of the year came, and all the money we had was the amount of our pledge to God. He won the victory, but more important we passed the test. We learned that God gives His wisdom and provides opportunities that far exceed our problems. We were beginning to learn how God grows His people to maturity. Praise His holy name.

God wants to be first in our lives, and growing faithful in the grace of giving provides a foundation for that. Why tithe? Because God's Word says we should. We may not be capable of living perfect lives in what we say and do, but in the matter of giving God the tithe of our income, we can be perfect. The tithe is God's, and as we tithe we grow in the grace of giving, which develops our basic spiritual maturity.

Tithing is about more than giving 10 percent of our income to God. Giving a tithe is an important part of the stewardship of our lives, but it is only the start. Tithing is not a scheme some preacher invented to raise money for a church. Rather, faithfully giving to God the first portion of our income is the beginning step in making Him the most important part of our lives. When our primary allegiance is to God, we learn to keep the first commandment, "You shall have no other gods before me" (Exodus 20:3). Old Testament tithing involved much more than a tenth of one's income. (See Leviticus 27:30–34, Numbers 18:21–32, and Deuteronomy 14:20–29, 26:12–19.)

Malachi chose to deal with the curse of not giving. He believed failure to give God a tithe was the same as robbing Him, since everything belongs to God by right of creation. Failure to tithe also shuts God's people off from His blessings. The prophet announced that God said, "Test me in this … and see if I will not throw open the floodgates of heaven and pour out a blessing" (Malachi 3:10). When we, the redeemed of the Lord, trust God's faithfulness to keep His word and "test" God's promises by obeying Him, we always come away with increased faith. That's because we have come face to face with God's promise and have experienced for ourselves that He can be trusted to keep His word.

When we believe God's Word and by faith obey Him even when we may not understand, His blessing flows into our lives. He opens the floodgates of heaven for His obedient children. What that cascade of blessings will be, only God knows. However, we can be sure that God will give us His very best and that our lives will be fuller and our witness of Him will be more powerful. Holy Father, give us your blessings so that we may be a blessing to others.

Jesus had much to say about honoring God with our gifts. Jesus validated the practice of tithing, but added that a believer should also be concerned about "justice, mercy and faithfulness" (Matthew 23:23). Tithing without knowing God and His divine love is pure legalism. I have known people who were as faithful as the sun rising in giving a tithe, but neglected to study God's Word. These same legalistic givers were the first to question the idea of trusting God's leadership in a faith venture or giving to missions. Where is our faith in God's leadership when we must have the money in the bank before we will trust God's provisions in any Holy Spirit-inspired endeavor?

The apostle Paul was collecting an offering for the Jerusalem church. That church was suffering financially because members had provided food and shelter for many of the people who were converted on the day of Pentecost when three thousand were saved. Paul urged the new mission churches to contribute to meet this financial need. The apostle wrote to the church in Corinth, urging members to finish their offering (2 Corinthians 8–9). To encourage them, Paul mentioned the church in Macedonia. Members there had given sacrificially, and Paul said of them "That they gave as much as they were able, and even beyond their ability" (2 Corinthians 8:3). Here was a small, struggling church that begged for the privilege of giving to the Jerusalem church.

However, the real key to their giving was that "They gave themselves first to the Lord" (2 Corinthians 8:5). This should be the motivation for every believer. When we give our whole selves to God, whatever we claim to own we also give to Him. When we give our all to God, we show Him that we love Him with all of our mind, soul, and body. Such a total commitment to God ensures that His blessings will surround our lives. What will these blessings be? How will God package them? Only He knows. However, we do know that He gave us His best in Christ and will continue to pour out His best gifts in our lives.

Tithing is a biblical command. My observation through the years has been that when the love of Christ lives in a believer, giving to the cause of Christ brings great pleasure and heaven's blessings. Paul calls giving to supply the needs of God's people a "service … also overflowing in many expressions of thanks to God" (2 Corinthians 9:12).

Inventor R. G. LeTourneau gave 90 percent of his income to the work of God. "The question," he said, "is not how much of my money I give back to God but how much of God's money I keep for myself." The tithe belongs to God. In fact, all we have is a gift to us from God. All God asks is that we give Him a portion of what He has so bountifully given to us.

Heavenly Father, we thank You for the gift of life, jobs, family, salvation, Your presence, and for watching over us every day of our lives. Thank You for food, shelter, salvation, and for the wonderful opportunity to work and make a living by Your help. We rejoice that we can say with the psalmist, "My help comes from the Lord, the maker of heaven and earth" (Psalm 121:2). Amen!

CHAPTER 6
THE WORD OF THE LORD

All scripture is God-breathed and is useful for teaching, rebuking, correcting and training in righteousness, so that the man of God may be thoroughly equipped for every good work.

—2 Timothy 3:16–17

. . . .

It is good to go to church whenever possible, and giving God His tithe is the right thing to do. However, it is possible to attend church every Sunday and Wednesday, to tithe, to sing in the choir, to teach a Bible class, and to serve on numerous committees and yet never grasp how much God loves us, nor truly worship the Almighty. Worship of God is an action inspired by the Holy Spirit as He opens our minds to the glory of God and moves our hearts to bow in wondrous adoration of our heavenly Father. I have known people who did many of the activities mentioned above but could have had their names on Jesus' description of the empty house (Matthew

12:43–45). They were people without the joy of God's Holy Spirit, and never demonstrated the loving compassion of Christ Jesus.

The prophet Isaiah had issues with people who said the right things but whose lives were poles apart from God's teachings. God said, "These people come near me with their mouth and honor me with their lips, but their hearts are far from me" (Isaiah 29:13). That is another way of saying they did not worship God, because they did not truly know Him. Knowing God begins with an understanding of His Word and how He has dealt with His people through the ages.

Here is an example of words and deeds that do not match. One Sunday afternoon, I stopped by to see my grandfather, who, in his final years, often attended church. Grandpa had collected some mules, which he was selling to farmers for their spring plowing. A prospective buyer stopped by and Grandpa said, "The mules are in the lot. Look at them if you want, but I do not do business on Sunday." I knew Grandpa well and saw his words were just a shield for the scam he planned to work on this unsuspecting buyer. He was attempting to create a false atmosphere of honesty. He would declare the mules to be sound, well broke, and often in matched pairs. These claims were just part of his sales pitch since he had collected the mules from wherever and whomever he could. The Word of God had not penetrated his heart, and therefore God's nature was foreign to him.

God's Word, read, meditated upon, and lived out, is the only way to receive the power needed for Christ-like living and to grasp the wondrous glory of God. It was three o'clock in the morning, and I was reading a western pocket novel in the smoke room at the paper mill when George, who operated a crane, entered. "Wren," he said, "if you would read the Bible half as much as you read that stuff, there is no telling what God would do with you." I ignored his comment, but felt a strange stirring for something more than I had ever imagined. In my heart, I knew those words of heavenly wisdom, spoken by a simple man of faith, were directed by God to guide me toward His purpose for my life.

At about this time, my brother and I decided to go into the service station business. Frank and I worked different shifts so we could switch off at the station. One evening two men who were bold witnesses for Christ pulled up for gas. I was filling Hilton Skipper's gas tank and was only half listening as he and his friend discussed a Bible verse. I became very much interested when Skipper said, "Well, I am sure a good Christian like Jack has a Bible in the office, and I will show you what I mean." I wished another customer would arrive so I could get busy pumping his gas, because I was ashamed to tell Skipper that I did not have a Bible with me.

I have often wondered if Skipper really wanted a Bible or if God had sent him as a special messenger to help me see the value of His holy Word. I can say without hesitation that there have been few days since then when I did not have ready access to a Bible. The Word of God changed who I was and why I was, and continues to adjust my life. Hallelujah!

My introduction to the Bible came when I was in the sixth grade. The new school year began in July, and the church next to the school always had Vacation Bible School when the new school year began. Students got prizes for memorizing Scripture verses. I won a fifteen-cent New Testament. My teacher, Marie Gattliff, wrote on the fly leaf words which, when I became a man, blessed my heart. She wrote

"This book is the anchor of hope. 'Tis the star that will shine through your life's darkest night."

She was correct about the value of God's Word. No self-help plan, no counseling technique, no macho lifting by the bootstraps, remotely compares with the transforming power of reading God's Word.

God had my attention and I became a Bible addict. I read it every chance I had. I would read at traffic lights, while Beth grocery shopped, and even during meals.

I decided to quit the paper mill and devote all my time to the service station. I faced financial difficulties, but this was a great move spiritually. Now I had time to read God's Word and to get involved in everything my church was doing, but most of all, God began to teach me to depend on His guidance.

Whatever the church asked me to do I did my best to carry out. I was assigned to lead the adult training union. I would begin the meeting with a devotional thought, and then others would share from the discussion guide. God would bring to my attention some part of the Bible for the devotional thought. Most of the time I knew very little about what I was sharing, but the amazing thing is how God used this to touch people's hearts. Attendance increased, and we began to pray for people who needed the Lord and to visit some who were on our hearts as we headed toward our spring revival. That spring our church experienced one of the greatest outpourings of the Holy Spirit's work I have ever seen. On the closing Sunday morning, so many people made decisions for Christ that they had to stand against the outside wall, circling the worship center. There was not enough room in the pulpit area.

During that week of revival, God spoke to my heart and said, "If you continue smoking, I cannot use you the way I want to." My most fervent desire was for God to use me any way He chose, and so in an instant I told Him, "I have tried to kick this habit without success. I will put cigarettes down, but You must take away the desire." With that, I flipped the pack in my desk drawer, and God removed the desire to smoke. It has never returned.

On the closing Sunday morning of the revival, I surrendered my life to God's call to serve Him as a preacher of the gospel. God had called me to be a minister when I was fifteen years old, and I had ignored Him until that morning. When I first felt God drawing me to serve Him, I knew nothing about church, the Bible, or how God worked in a believer's life. Not knowing God's nature, I thought that if I ignored him, He would go away. My surrender to God's call came because His Word had grown my faith and provided the avenue for the Holy Spirit to speak to my heart and open my life to God's will. My life turned in a new direction as I became consumed with the desire to know God's Word, to understand His will for my life, and by His grace to obey His voice.

The changes in my life were many. I gave up the service station, but continued to rise at four in the morning and study God's Word, a practice that still dominates my mornings. I prayed about a new job and felt that God had led me to a Pease Woodwork Company. However, the first day on the job, I felt like a fish out of water. There seemed to be no connection between the new direction my life was taking and this place of work. On the second day, I took my Bible and read it during lunch and on breaks. God's Word gave me peace along with the comforting sense of His presence.

The Bible helped me to find a haven of rest and peace in the amazing presence of Christ Jesus the Lord. The Word of God became the anchor that kept me in God's appointed place. The Bible remains my anchor. Reading God's Word at every opportunity was my practice during all my years at the woodwork company. Doing this kept my focus on God and helped me stay aware of His continual presence. As the apostle Paul says, "All scripture is God breathed and is useful for teaching, rebuking, correcting and training in righteousness, so that the man of God may be thoroughly equipped for every good work" (2 Timothy 3:16–17). There is no better way to manage life than to keep God's Word at the forefront of one's mind.

The second year I worked at Pease, another preacher was hired. Curtis Ramsey and I quickly became friends, and we read, prayed, studied, and discussed God's Word. In the next few years, God added to our number men who belonged to various denominations. The number of Bible readers grew so much that we moved into the break room and some others moved out. The agenda for our daily studies and discussions was, "What has God said to you from His Word?" Unless you were there, the scope of our daily discussions would be hard to imagine. I was learning how to witness to people who were not correctly handling God's Word and felt a spiritual emptiness.

A special incident lingers in my memory. One day the discussion turned to the subject of new birth. One man professed a religious belief that did not teach the necessity of a rebirth. I shared my testimony and asked him, "Have you ever had such an experience?" He answered no. "Why not" someone asked? He replied, "I do not know, but I will ask my priest."

The next day the man gave the priest's reply, which in no way matched Jesus' teaching in John 3 concerning the new birth. Following this discussion, the fellow said he would have to ask his priest about this discrepancy. However, the next day he told the group, "My priest said I should not talk to you people anymore." That day I knew that John 3 could turn the hearts of religious people who believed the Bible to be God's Word to a saving knowledge of Jesus' death on the cross. I have seen numerous lives turned to a saving faith when we studied John 3:1–16 around the kitchen table. Praise God.

Noah built the ark because God told him to. Abraham left his homeland and his family when God said he should. Moses met God in the wilderness, and at God's command, led the children of Israel out of slavery. Joshua led the Israelites into the Promised Land because he met the living God and experienced His holiness. Samuel heard the voice of the Lord, and this encounter transformed him into Israel's spiritual guide. Jeremiah, the weeping prophet, suffered severe persecution over God's word to him. Hosea sought out his wayward wife because God told him to do so.

The voice of God thundered, "This is my Son," at Jesus' baptism (Matthew 3:17), and the world was forever changed. Peter, Andrew, James, John, and the rest of the apostles left everything to follow Jesus when God in the flesh spoke to them. Paul stopped persecuting God's people and became a preacher of the gospel when God addressed him on the Damascus road. The list of people whose lives were changed by a word from God is endless.

All of these people heard God's message in some manner. The prophets were fond of saying, "The Word of the Lord came to me." In what way does God communicate today? Some say He speaks only through His written Word, but when God spoke in biblical times the story had not been written. Others suggest that God arouses people's awareness of special needs and that in this way they discover His purpose for their lives and ministries. However, there is evidence that God still speaks at full volume within the hearts and minds of believers.

I have never heard an audible word from God and do not know anyone who has, but in my spirit His voice has thundered many times. At times He has spoken so loudly that I have wondered how others could fail to hear the sound. Part of learning to obey God's will is coming to know the sound of His voice and separating it from the self-centered desires of one's own heart.

Beth and I once faced a decision about our life. She said, "I do not believe this is God's will for us." In my heart I knew she was right, but in my mind I was determined to do what I wanted anyway. Beth was right and I was wrong. That experience taught me to know the unique sound of God's voice, one of the most important lessons I have ever learned in my walk with God. Once we know the sound of His voice, we hear Him more clearly when we spend quality time with Him. After all, "We are His people, the sheep of His pasture" (Psalm 100:3). The only way for sheep to know the Shepherd's voice is to spend time with Him. Jesus said, "I am the Good Shepherd. My sheep listen to my voice; I know them, and they follow me" (John 10:14, 27).

God has sometimes whispered a command that led to an immediate ministry. At other times a Scripture verse seems to leap off of the page, and the Holy Spirit reveals that this is a "now" moment.

At other times the revelation is for a later teaching. However, all revelations by the Holy Spirit are for the rest of one's life.

In my early walk with God I asked, "How am I to serve you?" I was reading Isaiah 40:1 where God says, "Comfort, comfort my people." This was His answer to my prayer. Learning how to comfort God's people has remained my life's prevailing passion.

A close look at Isaiah 40 reveals that the prophet comforted God's people by showing that their seventy years of captivity was finished and that they were forgiven. The prophet pictured God as a tender, loving shepherd, embracing them in His arms. Isaiah also pointed out that God was mighty in power, that He rewarded obedience and punished disobedience, that He created the universe, that He knew of the people's suffering, and that if they waited in faith for Him to act, they would receive the peace of His deliverance. What a beautiful word picture we see when God says, "Those who hope in the Lord will renew their strength. They will soar on wings like eagles; they will run and not grow weary, they will walk, and not be faint" (Isaiah 40:31).

How can the Word of God create change in the hardest heart without intruding upon free will? God's Word has a powerful effect because it is extremely flexible and yet absolutely inflexible. It is inflexible in that sin is always sin, justice and righteousness are always demanded, and faithful obedience is always celebrated. Jesus is the one and only way to salvation and God is always true to His word.

However, God's Word is also exceedingly flexible. It must be flexible so that His message can be personalized to speak to the distinctiveness of every human situation. Consider the ways in which

God's Word is described. It is pictured as rain, snow, fire, a hammer, a light, and a two-edged sword, just to mention a few images.

The prophet Isaiah, in chapters 40–66, focused primarily on comforting and encouraging a people for whom God was opening a new day. God said His Word was like rain and snow (Isaiah 55:10). Isaiah believed that when God's Word was given it would in time have a positive effect and lead people to think as God thinks. The prophet therefore described God's Word as having the effect of rain and snow.

A farmer is filled with new hope when, during a long dry spell, a good rain falls on his crop. Keep in mind that rain works slowly to bring about new life. Rain waters the ground so that seed will spring up and grass will grow. Water is primary to human existence, and one of the first things space explorers look for is water because human life is not possible without it.

The Word of God, like water, is basic to our future with God. Jesus gave a beautiful picture of a believer's life in God's family when He said, "If anyone is thirsty, let him come to me and drink. Whoever believes in me, as the scripture has said, streams of living water will flow from within him" (John 7:37–38). Yes, He who is called the "Word of God" (Revelation 19:13) is the life-giving water without which no one shall see God. When we come to Jesus and drink from Him, His life flows from us, and He can use us to draw others to Him.

Isaiah also compared God's Word to snow. Though snow is frozen rain, it has a radically different effect on the earth. In the rolling hills of Kentucky where I grew up, when snow covered the ground any time after the first of the year, many people would sow grass seed on top of it. When the snow melted, the ground would be softened, the seed would sink into the soil, and when the sun warmed the earth, a beautiful crop of grass would emerge. So it is with God's Word. Sometimes His holy truth is immediately received, while at other times it gains slow and thoughtful acceptance. Rain and snow point to the Word's gentle persuasion. Rather than a rush to change, we see a slow, progressive awakening to a new truth, a gradual coming together of a new purpose in life, and a growing passion to know and to serve God.

The prophet Jeremiah described God's Word from a completely different point of view. Whereas Isaiah chose to comfort and encourage, Jeremiah's method was aggressive and filled with conflict. However, Jeremiah was dealing with people who ignored God, both His will and His Word. Therefore God said, "Is not my word like fire, declares the Lord, and like a hammer that breaks a rock to pieces?" (Jeremiah 23:29). Malachi said that fire refines and purifies (Malachi 3:2–3). The apostle Paul said that the fire of God's Word "will test the quality of each man's work" (1 Corinthians 3:13). This test is about the quality, not the quantity, of what believers do for Christ. It is not at all about salvation. Shadrach, Meshach, and Abednego were tested by fire when they refused to worship an idol (Daniel 3:16–17). Fire will devour everything that is not of God when testing time comes.

Jeremiah also said that God's Word is like a hammer. Just as continual pounding with a hammer turns the hardest stone into dust, the persistent reminder of God's truth demolishes the most stubborn will and tears down the wall of resistance to God.

I still rejoice when I see pictures of those unnamed protesters pounding the Berlin Wall and watching it crumble to earth, setting a people free. So it is with God's Word, and just as a hammer drove the nails into Jesus' hands and feet, so will the Holy Spirit keep hammering home God's beautiful truth into people's hearts and minds. When the people of God remain faithful to Him in a sinful environment, He will use their lives to hammer home His message in the sinful hearts of others.

I wish I had known better when I began my ministry what I have learned in the last few years. God's Word to me was "Comfort my people." What began in my early ministry remains my strongest gift. However, there are times when God calls us into situations that require more of Jeremiah's method than Isaiah's. I have never had a problem with Isaiah's method of comfort. However, Jeremiah's method has always led to difficulties and sleepless nights. I am not suggesting that what God led me to do was wrong, but I am saying Isaiah's method would have been more comforting to me during some tough years. Perhaps this insight will bring God's comforting peace to others who follow similar paths.

The author of Hebrews presented a different definition of God's Word when he called it a "two-edged sword" (Hebrews 4:12). Paul called God's Word "the sword of the Spirit" (Ephesians 6:17). A two-edged sword would cut both ways and was no doubt an effective instrument for slicing human flesh. The writer of Hebrews described how the Word of God can penetrate a human spirit so deeply that it slices its way into thoughts and attitudes. In joining God's Word to the Holy Spirit, Paul was saying that the awesome resurrection power of God uses the Word to pierce the deepest regions of our lives. What an awesome and wonderful picture! Jesus is sometimes called the Great Physician, and His Spirit wields God's Word to carve out sinful practices and ingrained attitudes. Glory! God's Word can radically change and strengthen our spiritual lives while we remain in the flesh.

God's Word began to so completely change my life that one of my family members said, "Beth has warped Jack's mind." This relative was right about the change but missed the mark about the agent of change. When you devour the Word of God, your life will change, and when the Word remains your steady diet the change will continue. Hallelujah!

The psalmist gave us two other wonderful ideas about God's Word. In Psalm 119:105, he said, "Your Word is a lamp to my feet and a light for my path." Who has not stumped a toe while trying to walk through the house without turning on a light? So it is with the person who has come to Christ for salvation but seeks to live for God without using His guidebook. Perhaps too many of us approach living for God the way I used to go about assembling my children's Christmas toys. I tried to put them together without reading the instructions. After all, I was mechanically gifted and could do this job all by myself. I should have gotten a patent for my efforts because sometimes what I put together did not look anything like the manufacturer's design.

Jesus spoke of the broad gate and the narrow gate. The broad gate may well be found without a light. However, the narrow way of God cannot be found or traveled without His guiding light. (See Matthew 7:13–14.) The apostle John called Jesus "the light that shines in the darkness" (John 1:5). Jesus lights the pathway out of the blackness of a lost soul into the loving arms of almighty God.

How are we to respond to the inflexible Word of God that never changes its message, but comes to us in ways that penetrate the heart and reveal the need for a changed lifestyle? The psalmist shared his method and it is a good one. He said, "I have hidden your word in my heart that I might not sin against you" (Psalm 119:11).

Heavenly Father, please help us to fill our hearts and minds with Your Word that we may live Christ-honoring lives and that we may "present ourselves to you as one approved, a workman who does not need to be ashamed, and who correctly handles the Word of truth" (2 Timothy 2:15). Amen!

CHAPTER 7

FRESH FLOWING WATER

Jesus said, "If anyone is thirsty, let him come to me and
drink. Whoever believes in me, as the scripture has said,
streams of living water will flow from within him."

—John 7:37–38

· ·

Knowledge of God's Word can be vast, commitments to church
activities praiseworthy, community service amazing, morality
above reproach, and church services well thought out, and still
church membership will continue to decline. How is this possible?
The answer can be found in 1 Corinthians 13:1–3. The apostle
says that believers can speak heavenly languages, understand the
mysteries of God, be filled with knowledge of God, have mountain-
moving faith, give generously to God's causes, die for their faith, and
still gain nothing. The reason, as the apostle John said, "You have
forsaken your first love" (Revelation 2:4).

We do well to remember that Jesus established the starting point for God's expectations of His people. Jesus said, "Love [*Agape*] the Lord your God with all your heart and with all your soul and with all your mind … love your neighbor as yourself" (Matthew 22:37, 39). *Agape* is God's kind of love for all people and is the measure of our love for Him and for others. God's love does not reject people, nor does it seek to control them. *Agape* love is self-giving for the good of others. Perhaps Paul summed it up best when he said, "Do nothing out of selfish ambition or vain conceit, but in humility consider others better than yourselves" (Philippians 2:3).

The Ten Commandments cover two areas of human life. They define the way God wants us to treat Him and others. God wants us to care about and relate to others in ways that show our respect and appreciation for them. However, our care for others will, in the final analysis, fall short until we learn to worship in the awesome beauty of God's holiness.

Worship, for many people, is difficult to define, let alone practice. Numerous writers have helped to enlighten believers in the art of worship. However, the Bible remains the best source for study and the only sure avenue to meet God in the splendor of His magnificent glory. The apostle John saw God being praised in heaven and knew this was what pleased Him on earth. How different our earthly existence would be if only we could keep our focus on God during tough times. The temptations of Jesus revealed the devil's plan for all of God's people. Jesus kept His cool during rejections, hostile debates, sinful displays, and even the agony of the cross. He never lost sight of the fact that God's desire was that all mankind recognize Him as the Son of God, sent to reveal the unending love of the Father.

David knew he needed to be in constant touch with God. He wrote, "I call to God, and the Lord saves me. Evening, morning, and noon I cry out" (Psalm 55:16–17). True worship of God is an attitude of the heart that spans every aspect of one's life. Worship that glorifies God lifts the worshipper, magnifies God's greatness and power, and expresses one's utter dependence upon Him.

I am amazed at how God in His loving care for His people gently draws us to places and people whom He uses to deepen our relationship with Him. Our pastor made an appeal to go hear a missionary from Africa speak. I have no memory of this missionary's work, but I have never forgotten the Bible lesson he taught from Genesis 12 and 13. He told of Abraham, whom I knew nothing about. I was particularly struck by the fact that Abraham built altars to worship God everywhere he went.

Abraham got to Canaan and the Lord promised to give the land to his descendants (Genesis 12). In response to God's promise, Abraham built an altar and called on the name of the Lord. However, like some of us, Abraham went beyond God's promise and seemed to stray from the Lord's plan for his life. When he returned to the Promised Land, Abraham went immediately to his altar and again called on the name of the Lord.

An altar was a place for sacrifice and recognition of God's presence; it was also a visible statement of gratitude. Calling on the name of the Lord involves worship and prayer. I wonder how many times we reach the end of our rope and in desperation cry out to the Lord God for deliverance, guidance, and wisdom. If we had been calling on God morning, noon, and night, the crisis might well have been avoided. Remember that Jesus taught his followers to pray, "Lead us not into temptation" (Matthew 6:13).

Everywhere Abraham went, he kept his relationship with God current by building altars and calling on the name of the Lord. Living as a minority in a strange land and an ungodly environment, Abraham knew his survival depended on God. We can learn how to manage life by studying the crisis in Abraham's life. He heard and followed God's call to a special place (Genesis 12). He kept worship of God active by always building altars (Genesis 12:7, 13:4). He gave God the credit for his every success (Genesis 14:20). He was honest with God and shared his doubts and fears (Genesis 15). God was Abraham's friend with whom he walked and talked (Genesis 18:16). Finally, Abraham passed his greatest test, withholding nothing, not even his precious son, from God (Genesis 22).

There are many similarities between Abraham's world and ours. Perhaps the most striking likeness is that present-day believers are, for the most part, surrounded by unbelievers. These unbelievers may not be physically dangerous in the United States, but they are surely indifferent to the gospel and pursue lifestyles that are clearly not of God. We need constant contact with God to avoid being sucked into the world's way of thinking, speaking, and acting.

Our church began a mission in another part of town. On a Wednesday evening, one of our deacons, Eldon White, led a Bible study in Revelation 4. He stressed the need to give God the glory for all success. The Holy Spirit highlighted Revelation 4:10 and the act of laying our lives and all we possess before the throne of God. Worship became more real to me as I pictured the throne of God the Father with Christ the Son beside Him and me with the privilege of placing everything at His feet. How enriched our lives are when we come boldly into the Father's presence, bow before Him in humble adoration, and give everything we have and who we are to Him as praise for His gracious love and goodness! Hallelujah, what a Savior!

God was changing me, my deep desires were shifting, and I had come to a place in life where I wanted to worship God two times on Sunday and be free to attend Bible study on Wednesday. Shift work in the paper mill hindered my heart's hunger. I still recall driving down the street to my house one Sunday afternoon after finishing my day at the mill and having missed the morning worship. My heart was heavy and I whispered to God, "Please help me get to the place where I can give You more of my life and be free to worship You all day every Sunday." God heard my plea and within a year I left the paper mill. However, a word of warning is in order because major changes in life will bring unimagined new struggles, difficulties designed by God to grow his child into a useful servant.

We are told, "Be careful what you ask for. You may get it." I say, "No. Go for it," because the joy of knowing the power of "Christ's resurrection and the fellowship of sharing in his sufferings" (Philippians 3:10) is worth it all.

I asked God to help me be free to worship Him all day Sunday. This prayer revealed my spiritual immaturity. At that point I did not know that God wanted not only Sunday, but all of the days of my life. Of course God wants His people to worship on Sunday, but He also wants His people to worship Him before sunrise and all through the day until sleep comes. I have found great value in welcoming the dawn and finishing the day by thanking God for the day's blessing as I snuggle into my pillow. David wrote, "Evening, morning, and noon I cry out ... and he hears my voice" (Psalm 55:17).

When thoughts of God drift in and out of our minds during the day and we are conscious of His presence with us, the day can end with a comforting sense of His peace. As the psalmist said, "God, you have made known to me the path of life; you will fill me with joy in your presence" (Psalm 16:11).

David's song of praise found in 2 Samuel 22 and Psalm 18 is among hundreds of Scripture passages that encourage worship of God and lead to adoration of our heavenly Father. David's song of praise to God reveals the attitudes required for true worship: reverence (vv. 1–4, 8–20), humility (vv. 26–30), submission (vv. 22–25), thanksgiving (vv. 31–43), and rejoicing (vv. 44–51). Jesus declared that God seeks such worship (John 4:24). [2]

To treat God with reverence is to accent the difference between His holiness, His complete otherness, and our sinful nature. God visited Abraham's tent and "Abraham fell face down" (Genesis 17:3). Moses turned aside to inspect the burning bush, and God told him, "Take off your sandals, for the place where you are standing is holy ground" (Exodus 3:5). When we find ourselves in God's holy presence, we instinctively cry out with Simon Peter, "Go away from me, Lord; I am a sinful man" (Luke 5:80. To revere Him is to call on the Lord, who is worthy of praise (2 Samuel 22).

Humility is the attitude that knows we cannot make ourselves sinless, that life and opportunity are God-given, that success and

---

2   See Disciple Study Bible: New International Version, Holman Bible Publishers, p-387.

happiness come from God, and that God cares for all people and watches to see how we treat others. Thus the apostle Paul could say, "Do nothing out of selfish ambition or vain conceit. Rather, in humility consider others better than yourselves" (Philippians 2:3). A good friend shared this story. One of his clients was in the office and mentioned that his feet were hurting. My friend knelt in front of him, removed his shoes, and rubbed his feet to relieve the pain. This man, secure in himself, is an example of a humble servant who places a high value on others.

There is great spiritual value in submission to the Lord. Yielding to God's will may not deliver us from suffering the difficulties of life, but it will bring us into the safety of God's defensive provisions. Jesus is our best example of submission to God. Facing the stark reality of the cross, Jesus cried out, "My Father, if it is possible, may this cup be taken from me. Yet not as I will, but as you will" (Matthew 26:39). Submission to God's plan for our lives brings safety because He knows what is around the next turn and over the next hill, and He is a loving guide who can help us fix the past, manage the present, and secure the future.

I was once angry at my church, bitter in opposition, involved in sinful practices, and out of God's will. My son bought a Fiat car and got it stuck in loose ground. The thing caught on fire, and much of the wiring was burned. He needed wheels, so I took over his payments and gave him my old second car. I bought a Fiat repair manual, feeling quite confident that I could fix the electrical problem since God had taught me that I could depend on Him for help in managing such situations. For six weeks, every Thursday from early morning until late afternoon, I hung over the fender of that piece of junk and tried to repair it, but nothing I did fixed the problem. I suppose I had become so used to feeling like a failure and the burden of my anger had so clouded my thinking that I had grown accustomed to futility.

About mid-morning on the sixth day, like the Prodigal Son, I came to my senses and realized how far I had drifted from God. Hanging over that fender, I had a tearful reunion. "Father," I prayed, "forgive me for drifting into sin. Please fill my heart with Your peace. Be the Lord of my life again and show me how to love this church, to be free of sinful involvements, and to obey Your will." At that moment my life changed, and the car was as good as fixed. My eyes fell on the repair manual, and I realized that I had been on the wrong page. A praise report is in order. In fifteen minutes the car was running. No wonder I could neither fix the car nor effectively manage my church or my family. I was on the wrong page of life and out of fellowship with God. Submission to God's Holy Spirit turned the page in my life.

An old story teaches a great lesson. A Puritan sat down to his meal and found that he had only a little bread and water. His response was, "What, all of this and Jesus Christ too!" The Scripture instructs us to "Give thanks in all circumstances" (1 Thessalonians 5:18). Therefore, thank You, heavenly Father, for bringing me into Your family; for calling me into ministry; for the gift of Beth as a loving wife for more than half a century; for bringing Jan into my life as a loving wife in these declining years; for every church I have served; for Your daily provisions; for Your long-term guidance; for a place to live in comfort; for health; for the parents You chose for me and the healthy genetics I received from them; for the fact that You have numbered my days on earth; for the filling of the Holy Spirit; for Jesus, who suffered for my sometimes willful and always thoughtless sin; for Your Word that feeds my soul; for Your continual presence; for my children, grandchildren, and great–grandchildren; for friends who have loved me when I was unlovable, and for You, my heavenly Father, who knew my spirit before I became earthbound, who loved me then, loves me now, and loves me always.

If I could sing, I would spend my life singing Your wondrous praise. I wish I could write in a style that captured the imagination and inspired praise of the Father. What I am You know, and in the words of Paul, "By the grace of God I am what I am" (1 Corinthians 15:10). In the shadow of Your grace, I can only say thank You, Father, for never giving up on me and for loving me every day of my life. Heavenly Father, thank You seems so little to say, but You know my heart; it is Yours. So from what is Yours, I thank You, Jehovah Jireh (Genesis 22:14).

Nehemiah said it well. "This day is sacred to our Lord. Do not grieve, for the joy of the Lord is your strength" (Nehemiah 8:10). These words were spoken by God's man to a struggling people. How are we to manage the difficulties of life? Shall we approach the day with a sour face and a heavy heart? Not if we want to win God's victory. Paul in prison said, "Rejoice in the Lord always. I will say it again: Rejoice!" (Philippians 4:4). We can approach life joyfully when we keep our focus on the Lord and not on our problems. By the power of the indwelling Holy Spirit, we can contrast the size of our difficulties with the greatness of God. He who created the universe, who by His power raised Jesus from the grave, is in no way limited by anything earthly. Therefore the way to manage day-to-day life is to rejoice in the love of Christ, to chill out in the presence of the Holy Spirit, and to worship the Father, because He is worthy of our highest praise.

I was jogging early one morning before daylight. The deep sky had no end, and it seemed I could almost touch the stars. For more than thirty minutes I had been joyfully praising God because of His Word, which says, "When I consider your heavens … what is man that you are mindful of him … you made him a little lower than heavenly beings and crowned him with glory and honor … you made him ruler over the works of your hands" (Psalm 8:3–5). I was in the midst of praise when I stepped on a rock and turned my ankle. At that moment a dog began barking. I was suddenly thrown into a cross-fire. I could throw rocks at the barking dog, I could sit down on the road and try to soothe the pain in my ankle, or I could lift my hands in praise for God's wondrous grace. I ignored the dog, limped on through the pain, and rejoiced in God's presence, which was even more real.

Nearly every day we will face the choice of being weighed down by the difficulties of life or of being lifted up. We must allow praise of God to guide us through the twists and turns of life. The choice, by God's grace, is ours.

It is spiritually profitable to devote a special time to be alone with God so that the Holy Spirit can open our hearts and minds to His awesome truths. Every follower of Christ would do well to cultivate the discipline of spending quality time alone with God as early in the day as possible. Prime time spent with God must become such a vital part of our spiritual lives that to miss meeting with Him leaves us with a sense of incompleteness. The more we spend time with

God the greater our hunger is to know Him better. Knowing God moved Paul to learn even more, and so he would say, "I want to know Christ Jesus and the power of his resurrection and the fellowship of sharing in his sufferings" (Philippians 3:10). Until we cry out for His guidance and help, we may never know the miracles God can work in our lives.

When we take God into the workplace, there will be many opportunities to seek His guidance and to praise Him for the success we achieve. I was operating a boring machine that was performing poorly. The bit boring the latch bolt hole was drifting and left a gap when the latch bolt was put in place. I knelt in front of the tool cabinet and prayed, "Lord, show me how to fix this problem, and I will tell everyone who passes by of Your help." God revealed to me two simple ideas that should have been evident, and the problem was solved.

The first person to come by was the plant manager. I thought, *O boy!* He asked, "What did you do?" With my heart in my throat, I said, "I prayed about it, God gave me two ideas, and they fixed the problem." He looked at me for a long time, then said, "I am glad we have someone here who can pray."

In the next few years I was moved from one machine to another, and each time God gave me the wisdom to fix problems and improve production. My last assignment was the most important to the company and by far the toughest. I was moved to a large press that was operating at about 70 percent efficiency, and the rejects required a number of men to make repairs. We made some progress, but the primary problem remained. The press was supposed to suction the metal door skin-flat, but too many of the completed doors came out of the press with large creases that had to be repaired by hand, and this was quite expensive.

I was eating lunch when God revealed the solution to me. That afternoon I made good products and bad ones whenever I chose. I notified the foreman that the problem was solved. The next morning the CEO and the rest of management gathered to see if my report was true. I made a good run and then told them I would return the press to the way it was before. Following several demonstrations of good and bad products, the plant engineer, a former NASA designer, asked, "Okay, what did you do? And I do not want to hear this 'I prayed' business." Ed and I had been down this road before, so I smiled at him and said, "Well Ed, whether you like it or not, I prayed and God gave me the answer."

When we begin the day with God and spend it with Him, He will bless us with His abiding presence and give us His wisdom for every life situation. He will do this because He wants to get His message outside of the church walls. Who else can He use but His people? God's message won't be heard or seen outside of the church building until His people take Him to the places where they spend most of their waking hours.

Heavenly Father, help us to keep You in the daily mix of our lives. Teach us how to ask for Your help in all things, both small and great. Amen!

CHAPTER 8

THE ASSIGNMENT

Jesus said, "The harvest is plentiful but the workers
are few. Ask the Lord of the harvest, therefore, to
send out workers into his harvest field."

—Matthew 9:37–38

· ·

My grandfather, O. T. Allen, a Pentecostal preacher of forty-
four years, was hospitalized with pancreatic cancer. I was
on my way to preach and went by the hospital to check on him.
"Grandpa, is there a Scripture I can read for you?" I asked. "Yes,"
he said. "Read 2 Timothy 4:1–8." I read the passage and Grandpa
said, "The first paragraph is for you and the second one is for me."
Grandpa Allen went to be with the Lord that Sunday night.

The last words of a dying grandparent linger throughout one's
life. They take on eternal significance when coupled with God's
Word. Grandpa Allen put the Word of God in my mind, but the
Holy Spirit burned it into my heart. The verse "Preach the Word,

do the work of an evangelist and discharge all the duties of your ministry" (2 Timothy 4:2) consumed my waking moments for many days. I have often asked myself, *When the end of my life comes, will I have fought the good fight, will I have finished the race, and will I have kept the faith?* (2 Timothy 4:7). Yes, I will, by the wondrous grace of our heavenly Father.

I have come to realize that God used many teachable moments in my life to bring me to a place of faith and commitment so that my heart would be prepared for His final series of lessons. The previous seven chapters of this book are based on life experiences in which God spoke to my heart and moved me one step closer to understanding His plan for my life. With each of those life-changing experiences, God offered new revelations that prepared me to reach people for Christ. The apostle Paul wrote to the Galatian church and said, "You were running a good race" (Galatians 5:7). But at an earlier point in my Christian life, I was not running with Jesus in his kingdom-building race.

The gospel of Matthew records that Jesus' first words to His disciples were, "Come, follow me, and I will make you fishers of men" (Matthew 4:19). A successful fisherman uses a variety of bait. The lure that will attract a bass will never work on a catfish. When Jesus said, "I will make you fishers of men," He meant that when we follow Him and let Him lead us where, when, and how He chooses, we will be His disciples. This discipleship will produce an enduring lifestyle that the Holy Spirit will use to show the love of God in Christ.

The word *make* in Matthew is *poieo* in the Greek translation. *Poieo* puts in motion a process that brings into being a way of life that takes on an existence all its own. Consider how following Jesus and learning from Him changed the apostles into men whose second nature was to think and act like Him. Jesus showed that the process of *poieo* belonged to God when He said, "You cannot make one hair white or black" (Matthew 5:36). In addition, "Jesus appointed [*poieo*] twelve, designating them apostles" (Mark 3:14), and they never stopped being apostles. Paul reminds us that whatever or whoever we submit to becomes our master. In Christ we "have been set free from sin, and have become slaves to righteousness" (Romans 6:18). Jesus has freed us from ourselves, and He asks us to give ourselves to Him so He can make us worthy disciples.

Jesus spoke of the need for a "new birth" to enter heaven. To be born into the world means the life in us will eventually take on its own existence. Our attitude and way of life determine the kind of people we become. When we dwell on anger, our second nature will be to respond to every situation with anger. The same principle holds true with *poieo*. What Jesus begins in us will, as we follow Him, become the main thrust of our lives. The Christian lifestyle will become our second nature.

Writing to the church in Philippi, Paul said that God "who began a good work in you will carry it on to completion" (Philippians 1:6). God uses worship in the Spirit, Spirit-led Bible study, and praying in the Spirit to grow His followers into believers whom He can use in His kingdom work. Keep in mind that "It is God who works in you to will and to act according to his good purpose" (Philippians 2:13).

Faith in God's transforming power is the bedrock on which He builds in developing a believer's ministering skills. My first lesson in being an effective witness for Christ came when the Southern Ohio Baptist Association sponsored a men's meeting and Dr. Carl Hunter was the speaker. Hunter quoted Romans 1:16, which says, "I am not ashamed of the gospel, because it is the power of God for the salvation of everyone who believes." This man of God quoted God's Word, and the Holy Spirit used this passage to capture my heart and to control my thinking for months. Hunter never knew how the Holy Spirit used his quotation of Scripture to speak to my heart and to convince me that God had the power to change lives. This verse brought me to a place where I believed God had the power not only to change lives, but to make me a useful witness for Christ.

Self-confidence is important to success in life. Bookshelves are filled with self-help suggestions. Perhaps they serve a worthwhile purpose; however, for the disciple of Christ, self-confidence must take a back seat to Christ-confidence. Meditating on Romans 1:16 over an extended period gave me both. God's Holy Spirit taught me to believe in His power beyond measure, and the spin-off was that He made (*poieo*) me into a bold, fearless witness. I came to believe that God could use me to witness in any situation or environment. What He did for me He can do for anyone who allows Him to be the almighty God He is.

God speaks through his people to touch others, and we may never know what He does with our words and actions. However, we must remember that God expects us to conduct ourselves in such a way that He can use what we say and do to encourage others to want Him in their lives.

The second step in my learning to witness for Christ came when my church taught Dr. C. E. Autery's book on soul winning. All that I remember about that book study was a story Autery told about a man who came to him and said, "Doc, I need help. I do not love lost people. I wish I did. What can I do?" Autery said, "Tell Jesus about it." I felt the same way at the time. I knew God wanted me to tell others about Him, but I had no conviction about doing so. I was not in the least troubled that people without Jesus as Savior were on their way to hell. I confessed my lack of concern to God and asked Him to help me love others as He loved them. True to His promise, Jesus taught me to care for the spiritual condition of people.

The third lesson in learning to witness to Jesus' power to save did not go well because I ran ahead of God. I decided to share the gospel with a man I knew, and the experience left me feeling somewhat like the seven sons of Sceva must have felt. These men sought to cast out a demon without accepting the leadership and power of the Holy Spirit (Acts 19:13–16). When I finished my presentation to Mr. X, he leaped to his feet and said, "If we both died right now, you would beat me to hell by five minutes." I never saw him again!

This experience affected me in two ways. First, I had to examine my life and question the things I did and said. Second, I realized I had run ahead of God. Like the disciples in Mark 9:14–29, I had neither the knowledge nor the power of God to share Jesus with lost people, because "this kind can come out only by prayer" (Mark 9:29). Fear of failure hung over me like the mantle of death.

Lesson four in the learning process happened with a man I came to know at the Pease Woodwork Company. Ed had worked at an atomic plant and had a cough that rattled of death. He entered the hospital and asked me to come see him. I arrived planning to ask him about his relationship with Christ, but I was so filled with fear that I could not bring myself to mention his spiritual condition. Following a sleepless night, I returned to the hospital. Armed with my Bible and a soul-winning tract, I promised God I would talk to Ed that day. When I arrived at Ed's room, an aide was washing the bed. I asked if he had been moved to another room. "Are you a relative?" the aide inquired. "No. Just a friend whom he asked to come and visit him," I replied. "I am sorry," the lady said. "Your friend died this morning."

I left that room blinded by tears and filled with a sense of having failed both God and Ed. I promised God, "This will never happen again." From that moment until now, I have grabbed every opportunity either at work, in the checkout line at the grocery store, in a hospital room, or on a plane to turn the conversation to Jesus.

My fifth lesson came when our church started a mission in another part of town, which grew into Rolling Hills Baptist Church. Every Saturday a number of us visited homes in the community, inviting people to church. I came to know a family that had no church home, and I asked if I could tell these people about Jesus. They said yes. I marked verses in my Bible, memorized key questions, and thought about how to move from Romans 3:23 to 6:23, then Romans 5:8 on to 10:9-10, closing with Romans 10:13. However, fear was still my problem. As I shared the story of Jesus, sweat soaked my shirt and ran down under my arms, and I had to keep mopping my brow. Hallelujah, this was victory day for me, because that day Jesus overcame the fear that had immobilized me and had kept me from sharing the gospel message.

Lesson six came when my wife Beth and I changed churches. A friend of mine, James Baughman, was pastor at Allison Avenue Baptist Church. Jim asked me to lead Thursday night visitation. One Thursday lingers in my memory. The night was so cold that the snow crunched at each step. I visited my first cousin's husband

Earl, and he accepted Christ. The following spring, my pastor was in revival. I preached for him, and Earl made a public profession of his faith in Jesus as Savior and Lord. Hallelujah! Words cannot adequately express my joy in the Holy Spirit when Earl walked the aisle. From that day until now, every time I have preached or taught, I have expected someone to make a profession of faith or some other meaningful commitment to Christ.

Seven is said to be a complete number. Call it what you will, but for me it was the final step God used to train me to be an effective witness to Jesus' power to save. The brotherhood department of the Ohio Baptist Convention sponsored a soul-winning conference. The focus of that Friday evening and Saturday morning retreat was an overview of Nelson Tull's book *Christian Witnessing*. The book contained only thirty-two pages, but was filled with suggestions for study and memorization that transformed my life. The Holy Spirit used this book to introduce me to Scripture passages and show me how to present Christ as Savior and Lord. That summer I memorized more than a hundred Scripture verses, and I had a firm command of at least five different plans to share the message of Jesus' offer to save.

This same year our association promoted a county-wide revival. As usual, counselors were trained to work with each person who made a decision. On one such evening I was paired with a teenage boy. I used the book of Romans, and he accepted Jesus. What I did not know was that a crowd of people had gathered behind me to hear my presentation of Christ as Savior. Several people in the crowd were involved in a new mission church, and one man later told me that he said, "That is the man we need to lead our mission."

This was graduation day for me! Jesus had kept His promise. You see, the first disciples were not the only people to whom He said, "Come, follow me and I will make you fishers of men" (Matthew 4:19). The Lord also said those words to me, and He says them to every born-again believer. The new mission church called me to be its pastor.

When Beth and I went to the Winton Hills Baptist Mission, our arrival increased the adult membership to six, with about a dozen children also attending. From day one, the power of God was evident. The first person to publicly accept Christ was a teenage boy. I asked him what I had heard other preachers ask, "How do you come?" He answered, "I rode my bike." I knew then that God had better be in charge of this work, because He was dealing with a totally ignorant man. Despite my blunders, God continued to add people to the church almost every week. In slightly less than three years, He used us to grow the membership to about 150 people, to secure property, and to construct a first-unit building.

This church was, from the beginning, the work of the Holy Spirit. We planned a fall revival that perfectly illustrates how God worked. During the revival, the visiting preacher and I would make home visits each afternoon and evening prior to the nightly services. We went to one home, presented Christ, and two adults accepted Jesus. As we prepared to leave because it was church time, a teenage girl stopped me and said, "I want to become a Christian also." The song service was in full swing when the evangelist and I made it to church.

God gave me the awesome privilege of being His servant at Winton Hills Baptist Mission, which later became Hilltop Baptist Church. I now know what I didn't realize in those days—that throughout my life, God had been leading me to this appointed time and place. To God be the glory for the great things He has done!

Thank You, holy Father, for the priceless privilege of serving You. That remains my greatest joy. Please help all who serve Christ to be filled with Your gift of faith, to speak as Christ would, and to love as Christ loved. We humbly lift this prayer in the mighty name of Christ Jesus the Lord. Amen!

Jesus' first words to His disciples were, "Come, follow me, and I will make you fishers of men." The Lord's final words in Matthew were, "Go and make disciples of all nations" (Matthew 28:19). From His first encounter with His followers until His return to heaven, Jesus' goal for His disciples was to make them into men who could and would share the gospel. The gospel message is "that Christ died for our sins … that He was buried, that He was raised on the third day" (1 Corinthians 15:3–4).

The gospel of Matthew is only one of sixty-six parts of the Bible. From Genesis to Revelation, the Holy Spirit has designed the Word of God to lead people to know Jesus as Savior and Lord. Accepting Jesus as Savior is but the first step in discipleship. The goal of Scripture is to inspire all believers to tell others what Jesus has done and continues to do for them.

Matthew 4:19 records Jesus saying, "I will make you fishers of men." We have looked at the word *make* and the meaning of the Greek word *poieo* earlier in this chapter. Keep in mind that *poieo* is the work of God, and He stays at it until His followers become effective witnesses.

Sometimes a person is quickly led to Christ and the evangelist can move on to the next prospect. But moving on too quickly can create a problem. This used to be described in Baptist circles as "dipping them and then dropping them." The idea was that our major concern seemed to be getting people on our church rolls and then pursuing the next new convert.

There is much more to evangelism than leading a person to accept Christ. A few years ago a theme in evangelism was soul-winning and soul-building. When a new convert is reached, the work has only begun, because the person is a long way from being a mature believer.

When Jesus said, "Go and make disciples," He established the goal of all evangelism. "Make disciples" in the Greek is *matheteuo* (mah-they-tyoo-oh). This word reveals a new dimension in building the kingdom of God that occurs only in a continuing relationship. *Matheteuo* describes a lasting connection between the teacher and the pupil. In this relationship, not only does the pupil learn from the teacher, but a bond develops between them that leads the pupil to believe and to act like the teacher.

Jesus makes clear that in the process of discipling new believers there is no quick fix. He said, "Teach them to obey everything I have commanded you" (Matthew 28:20). It takes a while to teach everything Jesus commanded! He spent three years with the twelve, training them in kingdom principles. Also, following the great harvest of souls on the day of Pentecost when three thousand were saved, Scripture says of these new believers that "They devoted themselves to the apostles' teaching, and to the fellowship, to the breaking of bread and to prayer" (Acts 2:42).

Later, more were added to the church "and the number of men grew to about five thousand" (Acts 4:4). The church in Jerusalem continued to grow to the point where the Jewish leaders sought to destroy the Jesus movement. "A great persecution broke out against the church at Jerusalem, and all except the apostles were scattered throughout Judea and Samaria" (Acts 8:10).

Paul broke up the party and ran the disciples out of town, but they left with something they did not have when they arrived. These new converts had spent time with the apostles learning about Jesus, and when they left Jerusalem they apparently told everyone they met that they had found the Messiah, the Lord Jesus Christ.

Acts 8:4 says, "Those who had been scattered preached the Word wherever they went." Were all of these people preachers, or were they farmers, carpenters, wives, young people, students, and shopkeepers? The Jewish rulers sought to stamp out Christianity; they succeeded only in extending the witness of Jesus.

Acts 8:4 says that the scattered "preached," and some translations of Acts 8:5 say that Philip "preached." A clearer translation may be "evangelized" in verse 4 and "proclaimed" in verse 5. "Preached" in Acts 8:4 is *euaggelizo* in the Greek and means "to evangelize," telling the good news about Jesus on a personal level, one to one, with the intent of winning a convert. "Preached" in Acts 8:5 is *kerusso* in the Greek and describes a herald proclaiming a message. *Kerusso* means delivering a message to everyone within hearing, much like the town crier of old who went through the streets shouting out the news of the day. In this sense the preacher is a herald; he bears a message, repeating publicly what was told to him by the heavenly King and spoken to a gathering of people.

Philip, it seems, preached to a crowd, while the scattered believers shared one to one the good news about Jesus. The Holy Spirit grows the Lord's people to become witnesses for Christ. Witnessing about Jesus is simple; just tell others what He means to you and what He is doing in your life.

Many good Christians sincerely believe that only preachers or other spiritually gifted believers can witness to Jesus. Satan has been promoting this myth from the beginning to spread the idea that only certain people are expected to share the gospel. It is true that within the body of believers "we have different gifts according to the grace given us" (Romans 12:6). It is also true that some in the body are especially gifted in leading people to accept Christ. This does not excuse born-again believers from living Christ-honoring lives and telling their friends and neighbors why they live the way they do. God uses many different people and messages to win unbelievers to Himself. Living Christ-honoring lives in one's community and work environment is witnessing to the glory of Jesus and is exactly what Paul meant when he wrote, "As the Lord has assigned to each his task. I planted the seed, Apollos watered it, but God made it grow" (1 Corinthians 3:5–6).

Let me illustrate this biblical principle. A woman whose husband was not a believer joined the church where I was serving as pastor. Soon after joining, she asked if I would visit her husband. She said, "For years I have had every visiting evangelist and pastor talk to him about becoming a Christian and he is still lost. Would you please come see him?" This man worked the second shift and left for work at three in the afternoon. I arrived at his home at 1 p.m. and welcomed him into God's family at 1:30 p.m. Many of God's servants had planted a seed of faith, others through the years had witnessed to him, and God used me to harvest this soul for Christ. That is the way God gets His kingdom work done.

God uses many people to bring to spiritual maturity those who follow Him, and this is Paul's message in 1 Corinthians 12:12–26. The apostle in this passage compares spiritually gifted believers to members of a body. The church is the body of Christ, and for the body of Christ to be strong and offer a viable witness in the world, all members must serve in the way God has spiritually gifted them. God in His wonderful wisdom has given every believer at least one spiritual gift that when properly understood and persistently developed provides a starting point for witnessing to Jesus' power to change lives.

We are born into this world with certain God-given abilities, and when we become followers of Christ, God adds spiritual gifts to our natural abilities. First, there are natural abilities, those God-given talents that help us become doctors, lawyers, merchants, chiefs, great cooks, or designers. Natural abilities provide us with insight so that we find in certain situations that we know that we know, though we may not know how we know what we know.

When we use the natural abilities that God gives us, some things are easy to handle. My daughter Amy is quite creative. When she was five years old she loved to spend time with me in my shop. She would take blocks of scrap wood and nail them together in unique ways. Her specialty in those early years was making step stools. We were on our way to church one Wednesday evening and came up behind a truck loaded with two-inch lumber. Amy leaned over the seat and said, "Daddy, if I had that lumber I could really make some stools." She could see the possibilities in that load of lumber.

The same is true in spiritually gifted believers. When we allow Jesus to make us in His image, with the spiritual gifts that He gives, it becomes second nature to see the spiritual possibility in any situation.

Here is an illustration. You will recall that my brother and I owned a service station. During that time I developed some minor skills. In my first pastorate I was visiting door to door and came upon an old man who was working on his car. He was trying to adjust the carburetor but was having no success. We talked for a bit and I said, "I have some experience in this area. Could I try to adjust it for you?" The engine quickly leveled out, and I made a new contact with whom I would, in the weeks to come, share the story of Christ Jesus. The old gentleman was Matthew Giltner. At seventy-seven, he became the oldest person I ever led to Christ. It was my great honor to baptize Matthew and welcome him into the family of God. I had learned to tune cars in the service station business. Could that have been God's plan all along to reach Matthew with the gospel? Reaching just one person for Christ is worth whatever it takes!

Are you a believer in Christ? Then you too are to tell His story by living your life for Him. Perhaps the problem is that we, the church leadership, have not sufficiently taught God's Word concerning spiritual gifts. These gifts are God-given tools that help a believer take part in God's work in others' lives. The Bible says that God gives spiritual gifts to His people as He chooses and that "we have different gifts, according to the grace given us" (Romans 12:6). The list of spiritual gifts in Scripture can be found in Romans 12:6–8; 1 Corinthians 12:4–11, 28; Ephesians 4:11, and 1 Peter 4:10–11.

The Bible mentions more than twenty spiritual gifts. They serve specific purposes in reaching and discipling God's people. There are gifts of grace for serving, gifts of ministries within the body of Christ, and supernatural gifts that go beyond human abilities. Finally, there are equipping gifts that build up the body of Christ. The listing of these gifts in no way limits God's power to further equip His people with specialized gifts to share the gospel in such a way that it can be understood in every evolving culture.

Is Jesus still working on you, growing you in Christ-likeness so that you immediately see the possibility of using your God-given spiritual gift to touch lives for Him? We may see ourselves as fishers of men, soul winners, cultivators, evangelists, teachers, pastors, servants, laypeople, housewives, or just ordinary Christians. How ever we describe ourselves, the skills we possess for living life are God-given and are meant to be used to bring Him glory and to build His kingdom. God expects His people to spread the gospel of Jesus to every corner of their neighborhood, city, state, nation, and world. He has assigned every believer the responsibility of working in His harvest and "shocking the wheat," because the fields truly are ready for harvest. All God needs to change lives on a grand scale is for His followers to faithfully tell their life stories by the way they live and what they say.

C. Roy Angell shared a story he received from Dr. John Maguire concerning a Florida state high school track meet. One of the schools had a most promising distance runner, and the rumor was that the state record for the mile might be broken. All eyes were on the tall athlete as the runners gathered at the starting line. Maguire said, "I saw at the far end of the starting line, a boy who in every way was in sharp contrast to the promising miler. He was small of stature, his shoulders were bent, his chest was hollow, and even his legs were not straight. I wondered why in the world a school would put a boy like that into the mile race to run against such a splendid athlete."

The race began and it was soon evident that there was only one runner. Other runners quickly dropped out of the race, and the super athlete sprinted for the finish line and broke the state record.

The race was over, and officials were bringing out the hurdles to set up for the next race. Suddenly one of the judges yelled, "Get those hurdles out of the way. This race is not over. Look!" Around the turn came that little boy, panting for breath and staggering. He dragged himself across the finish line and fell face down on the cinder track. One of the judges ran to him, turned him over on his back, took out his handkerchief, and wiped the blood off of the boy's face. The judge asked, "Son, why didn't you drop out back yonder? What are you doing in a mile race anyway?"

The little boy said, "My school had a good miler, but he got sick and couldn't run. The coach had promised to have a man in every event, so he asked me if I'd come and run the mile."

"Well, son," the judge continued, "why didn't you just drop out, quit way back there?" The boy answered, "Judge, they didn't send me here to quit. They didn't send me here to win. They sent me here to run this mile, and I ran the mile." [3]

3   C. Roy Angell, *God's Gold Mines* p-101-02 (Broadman Press, 1962)

Heavenly Father, help us to know You better. Open the eyes of our hearts so we can understand the hope to which You have called us. Show us the glorious inheritance You have planned for us, and reveal to us your incomparably great power in everyone who believes. Lead us to people whom You have prepared for Your message, and anoint us with Your power for Your glory and their salvations. Amen!

CONCLUSION

. . . .

Jesus said, "The harvest is plentiful, but the workers are few. Ask the Lord of the harvest, therefore, to send out workers into his harvest field" (Luke 10:2). Now go! "As God's fellow workers we urge you not to receive God's grace in vain. I tell you now is the time of God's favor, now is the time of salvation" (2 Corinthians 6:1–2). Now it is our turn to "shock the wheat," to get involved in reaching people for Christ, because the need to know Jesus as Savior and Lord has never been greater.

May almighty God, the God of Abraham, Isaac, Jacob, John, Peter, and Paul, anoint us with desire, wisdom, and power to live as God's grace inspires us. Lord Jesus, renew our spirits, fill our hearts with your love, open our eyes to the spiritual needs around us, and capture our wills that we will cry out with Isaiah, "Here am I. Send me!" (Isaiah 6:8). Now is our time; this is our place; we have our assignment. Help us, heavenly Father, to go with You into Your harvest field and to live godly lives for Your glory so others can see Jesus in us and want Him in their lives. Amen!

CPSIA information can be obtained at www.ICGtesting.com
Printed in the USA
LVOW11s0956131114

413478LV00001B/30/P

9 781462 739110